THE BEGINNINGS OF ENGLISH
LITERARY PERIODICALS

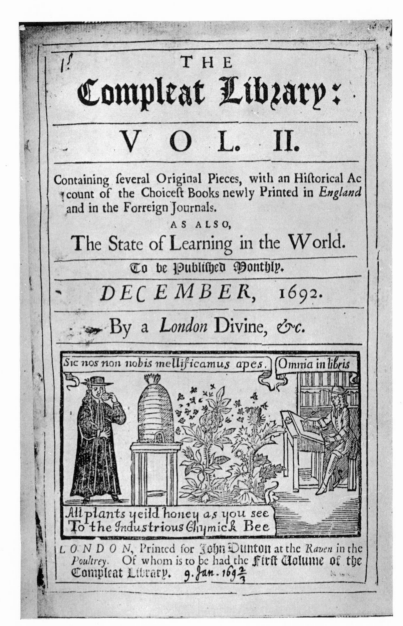

THE

Compleat Library:

VOL. II.

Containing feveral Original Pieces, with an Hiftorical Ac
count of the Choiceft Books newly Printed in *England*
and in the Forreign Journals.

AS ALSO,

The State of Learning in the World.

To be Publifhed Monthly.

DECEMBER, 1692.

By a *London* Divine, *&c.*

Sic nos non nobis mellificamus apes. | Omnia in libris

All plants yeild honey as you see
To the Industrious Chymick Bee

LONDON, Printed for John Dunton at the *Raven* in the
Poultrey. Of whom is to be had the Firft Volume of the
Compleat Library. 9. *Jan*. 169 2/3

ONE OF THE MOST NOTABLE LITERARY JOURNALS OF THE
SEVENTEENTH CENTURY

THE BEGINNINGS OF ENGLISH LITERARY PERIODICALS

A Study of Periodical Literature
1665 — 1715

BY
WALTER GRAHAM

OCTAGON BOOKS

A DIVISION OF FARRAR, STRAUS AND GIROUX

New York   1972

Reprinted 1972
by special arrangement with Mrs. Walter J. Graham

OCTAGON BOOKS
A DIVISION OF FARRAR, STRAUS & GIROUX, INC.
19 Union Square West
New York, N. Y. 10003

LIBRARY OF CONGRESS CATALOG CARD NUMBER: 74-159190

ISBN 0-374-93229-8

Printed in U.S.A. by
NOBLE OFFSET PRINTERS, INC.
New York, N.Y. 10003

PREFACE

FEW things are more ephemeral than periodical publications. Of the many thousands of copies issued during the seventeenth century, a comparative few have been preserved. These have survived more by accident than design, and are to be found in the collections made by such men as George Thomason, Charles Burney, John Nichols, and Thomas Hope. From the number of such serials in the libraries of England, the chronicle of the newspaper press has been written by Andrews, Grant, Fox-Bourne, Williams, and others. A much more interesting story has been neglected — which may likewise be gleaned from the meagre records — the story of the development of the literary periodical, involving, as it does, all that English writers and readers have been entertained by and believed and hoped. The development of the English literary periodical, in the period least known to modern readers, is therefore the subject of this study.

Several streams of tendency combined to produce the literary journal or magazine we read today. Of these, remote beginnings may be found in advertisements for books, abstract serials, periodical catalogues, pamphlets, entertaining features in newspapers, and half-sheet folios of political satire which appeared before 1700. All these origins cannot be considered at once, although contemporaneous. So, in order to present the facts in something like a chronological sequence, the arbitrary division which follows may perhaps be justified. Early periodicals that contributed to the "literary" tradition are separated, before 1709, into two classes — those of a learned nature, and those published only for the entertainment of the reader. It was mainly from these two types that the literary periodicals of the eighteenth century developed.

W. G.

CONTENTS

I.   THE LEARNED PERIODICAL 1
     De Sallo, De la Crose, and Dunton.

II. THE PERIODICAL OF AMUSEMENT 36
     Ned Ward, Peter Anthony Motteux, and
     Defoe.

III. SOME CRITICS AND REFORMERS 55
     The *Moderator* and Tutchin's *Observator*.

IV. THE " TATLER," " SPECTATOR," AND " GUARD-
     IAN " 61
     Steele and Addison.

ILLUSTRATIONS

One of the Most Notable Literary Journals of the
Seventeenth Century . . . . *Frontispiece*

A Little-Known Ancestor of the Modern Review . . . 26

The *Gentleman's Journal* was the First Magazine in a
Modern Sense 44

A Contemporary of Defoe's *Review* 54

The First Important Imitator of the *Tatler* 74

The Beginnings of
English Literary Periodicals

I

THE LEARNED PERIODICAL

THE earliest remote ancestors of modern literary journals were the book notices of the seventeenth century, appearing as the first advertisements in newsbooks.
Condemnations of works subject to Parliamentary investi-
gation followed, with puffs of propagandists; and later, occasional words of praise from the pens of licensers. An
isolated case of a book " this present day published " has
been found in the *Mercurius Britannicus*, as early as February 1, 1626, but it has little bearing on later reviews.
The expression of critical opinion began not earlier than
1646, when book notices were appearing with some regularity in the tiny serials of the day.

News matter and advertising were naïvely combined
at first, as in the *Perfect Diurnall of the Passages in
Parliament*, a weekly newsbook of importance, edited by
Samuel Pecke, who paused in his discussion of the victory
of Cromwell's army at Oxford, to recommend to his readers " a booke now in the Presse and ready to be published,
entitled *Magnalia Dei Anglicana, or England's Parliamentary Chronicles*, and the most exactest hitherto collected. . . ." This is a fair example of the way such
notices appeared up to 1646. Although book publishing
and book selling were only parts of a single enterprise,

1

few publishers made before 1650 any attempt to advertise their wares otherwise than by such an occasional news reference. And in each case the item-notice was written by the publisher of the book, or by another publisher who, for a religious or political reason, had an interest in it. During the 1640's the works of Milton, Davenant, Izaak Walton, Browne, and Cowley, were advertised to the world and "reviewed" in this manner; and not until 1650 or thereabouts did the book notices begin to resemble modern paid advertisements. Just before this change took place, such notices were most like later reviews. Soon after 1650 they were grouped on the last page of the paper and printed in smaller type than the news. By 1651 advertisements of other things began to appear; but books continued to make up most of the advertising as late as 1655, when Marchamont Nedham in his *Publick Intelligencer* separated the notices of books from those of quack medicines and other commodities.

Another ancestor of the literary periodical, one far more important than the early book notice, was the *abstract serial*. The publication of the *Journal des Savans* in Paris in 1665 not only gave an impetus to the issuing of periodicals both in Great Britain and on the Continent, but marked the beginning of a long line of serials devoted largely to the abstracting of books for busy readers. So important, in fact, was the *Journal des Savans* in this century, that some account must be given here of this French periodical, which flourished almost without a break for two and a half centuries, and of which Gibbon wrote in 1763: " I can scarcely express how delighted I am with this journal; its characteristics are erudition, precision, and taste. The father of the rest, it is still their superior."

The *Journal des Savans* may have been suggested by the publications of the *Bureau d'adresse* (1633–42) which gave the proceedings of conferences on literary and scientific matters in a serial work of Théophraste Renaudot, later the founder of the Paris *Gazette*. At any rate, in 1633, the historian François de Mézeray (1610–83) obtained a privilege for a regular periodical. His plan came to nought, and Denis de Sallo, Counsellor of the Parliament of Paris and a man of considerable learning, actually set up the first regular publication of this kind. From Sallo's personal habit of digest and commentary seems to have come the idea of a journal that should contain summaries of books; and as such the *Journal des Savans* first appeared. It was a twelve-page weekly, issued on Mondays. The " Imprimateur " of the first number (January 5, 1665) shows how much the purpose and content of later periodicals in England were anticipated.

The aim of this Journal being to give information concerning new happenings in the Republick of Letters it will be composed:

First, of an exact catalog of the principal books which are printed in Europe. We will not be content with giving simply the titles, as has been done hitherto by most bibliographers, but we will tell, moreover, of what they treated and in what they may be useful.

Second, when there shall die some person who is celebrated for his doctrine and his works, we shall praise him and give a catalog of his works, together with the principal facts of his life.

Third, we shall set forth the experiments in physics or chemistry which may serve to explain the effects of nature, the new discoveries in the arts and sciences, such as machines, and the useful or curious inventions which mathematics may develop — the observation of the heavens, those of meteors, and whatever new things anatomy may discover among the animals.

Fourth, the principal decisions of the secular and ecclesiastical tribunals, the decisions of the Sorbonne and other Universities in foreign lands, as well as in this country.

Finally, we shall try to so do that nothing may happen in

Europe worthy of the curiosity of men of letters which cannot be learned of in this Journal.

. . . .

. . . As for style, as several persons will contribute to this Journal, it will be impossible for it to be very uniform. But because this unevenness, resulting from the diversity of subjects as well as from those who treat them, might be disagreeable, we have requested M. de Hédouville to take the task of adjusting the material which shall come from different hands, so that it may have some proportion and regularity. Thus, without changing the judgment of such a one, he will take the liberty of changing sometimes the expression. He will join no party. This impartiality will doubtless be judged necessary in a work no less free from prejudice than from partiality.[1]

M. de Hédouville, who, as Sallo soberly declared, had undertaken to conduct the weekly journal, was Sallo himself under an assumed name — that of his butler, tradition has it. This incognito gave him a liberty of expression equal to that of Lockhart or Christopher North, nearly two centuries later. It led him to write in a tone often tart and stinging, and soon brought attention from "authority." In particular, his outspoken championship of Baluze and Launoy against the court of Rome was so offensive that Sallo lost his privileges, with the thirteenth number (March 29). Since he refused to continue his periodical under the surveillance of a censor, the enterprise was turned over to another, the Abbé Gallois, in January 1666. Abbé la Roque, who had formerly assisted Abbé Gallois, took it up from 1685, President Cousin from 1687, and from 1702 to 1792 it was edited by a commission of men of letters. Suppressed for a time, it was again issued in 1816 and following, under the auspices of the Institute. It is still in progress.

[1] Of course the idea of abstracting books was not original with Denis de Sallo. Photius of Greece, cir. 890 A.D., wrote in his *Myriobiblion* summaries of the works he read.

The *Journal des Savans*, as it was then called, was primarily an *abstract periodical* (*i.e.*, giving abstracts of books), the first of the *genre*. This fact deserves emphasis because of the long line of English serials that followed, in many cases devoted entirely to the abstracting of books. After the first few numbers of his journal, Sallo included original matter, in accordance with his plan. Undoubtedly the appearance of Henry Oldenburg's *Philosophical Transactions of the Royal Society*, which began in March 1665, had some effect on the Paris journal. The Royal Society had been founded a short time before this, an outgrowth of the interest in science of sorts, the "new philosophy," and the general desire for experiment and research. Men of letters were included at first, as is shown by Dryden's early election to the Society. Oldenburg had been secretary from the beginning. He began publishing the *Acta Philosophica Societatis Anglia* (the original title) in an endeavor to give "some account of the present undertakings, studies, and labours of the Ingenious in many considerable parts of the world."

Before his death in 1677, Oldenburg had not only edited 136 numbers of the *Transactions,* but had contributed a large number of original articles. Maty's *Index* to the *Philosophical Transactions* lists thirty-four studies of which he was author or translator. None of them were of a literary nature, of course. The importance of his work consists solely in the part played by the *Transactions* in the evolution of the "learned" periodical, which in turn had its important effect on the journal of criticism.

Appearing originally as a 16–24 page, monthly serial, the *Transactions* contained at first only original articles, in many cases signed by the writers. A page of wood-cut illustrations inset on a folded sheet was customary. This was probably imitated from the *Journal des Savans,* as the abstracts of scientific works which followed later undoubtedly were. The obligation was not one-sided, for after March, Sallo constantly quoted the English serial, usually including translations from it in a section termed *Extraits du Journal d'Angleterre.* After Oldenburg's death in 1677, his serial was edited by various hands until 1752, when a committee of the Society became responsible for it. Only during its early years was it of any real importance in the history of the literary periodical, or that phase of it concerned with reviewing. For it was the first *abstract periodical* in English.

In an age when publishers were invariably booksellers also, it was perhaps inevitable that the advertisements at the end of newsbooks or " transactions" should sooner or later become catalogues of books, issued as regular serials. The earliest book catalogue in England — Andrew Maunsell's in 1595 — and an annual catalogue of 1664, which did not survive the initial number, are worth noting. But the *Mercurius Librarius,* 1668, the so-called *Term Catalogue* of the London booksellers, was the first real example of the type. In a very limited sense only, it is entitled to be regarded as the first literary periodical published in England, and the " great-grandfather of the *Literary Gazette* and *Athenaeum."* The first number appeared in the Michaelmas Term, the projectors announcing that if it found encouragement it should be continued at the end of every term, *i.e.,* four times a year, in February, May, June, and November. The needed encouragement was furnished, and the *Term Catalogue* was issued in this manner until 1709.

The story of the founding and editing of this serial by the young stationers, John Starkey and Robert Clavell, has been well told in the introduction to the Arber reprint. It was a trade journal purely, for twenty or more booksellers, whose wares were listed and described under the headings: Divinity, Physick, Histories, Humanity, Players, and Books reprinted. As such, it was not of great importance in the development of periodical literature, although its appearance for so long a time seems to have had some effect on the form of succeeding publications of a more critical character.

Another *Mercurius Librarius,* or "a faithful account of all books and pamphlets published these last fourteen days," began on Friday, April 16, 1680. According to the prefatory statement in the first number, it was started because of the need of a weekly as well as a "term" catalogue, to serve the trade. It was promised to readers every Thursday morning, the contents limited to giving the title and design of each book and not attempting comment of any sort. The first number contained twenty-six short notices of books, with the name of the seller and the price of each. There are no records regarding its discontinuance, although it seems unlikely that it lasted long.

Following these, as it did, the *Philosophical Collections* of Robert Hooke, 1681–2, which ran through seven monthly numbers, although otherwise much like the *Transactions,* had something of the book catalogue character. Hooke had been a colleague of Oldenburg, having been appointed curator of experiments for the Royal Society in 1662, and succeeding Oldenburg as secretary in 1677. The aim of his work was "a candid commendation of useful discoveries." Each number of the *Philosophical Collections* consisted of about eight articles, on scientific subjects chiefly and signed by lettered authors like Edmund Halley, the astronomer, John Beaumont, or Dr. Frederick Slare. These were followed in the first number by accounts of new books and two advertisements for astronomical apparatus. Number two made no distinction between book notices and articles or abstracts. The title of a book was quoted in full at the head of each abstract, after the manner of the French journals, and each number was illustrated with a page of wood-cuts, similar to that which regularly appeared in the *Journal des Savans* or the *Transactions*.

But the *Weekly Memorials for the Ingenious*, which had begun in January 1682, was more like the *Journal des Savans* than any English serial that had preceded it. It began as a small weekly quarto of eight pages, printed for Henry Faithorne and John Kersey, and was made up, like its French model, of abstracts from foreign books or " transactions " from foreign journals, with, now and then, an original article. James Petiver has frequently been referred to as if he were the author. Undoubtedly, he wrote numerous papers on botany and herbs, but probably had no further connection with it. One of the Bodleian copies has " by Mr. Beaumont " written on the title page in faded ink. Probably John Beaumont was meant, a writer on supernatural subjects and scientist of some reputation. But by what authority the work may be assigned to him cannot now be determined. *Weekly Memorials* was conducted by the original author, until the seventh number had appeared. Numbers eight and nine were issued by the publishers, in spite of the withdrawal of the "author." Then there appeared the unparalleled spectacle of two periodicals with the same title, being issued by different publishers on the same day, March 20,. with identical letterpress — " No 1 " as published for R. Chiswell, W. Crook, and S. Crouch, and " 10 alias No. 1 " as printed for Faithorne and Kersey. From this point, the two *Weekly Memorials*, although practically the same in form, differed usually in contents. Numbers eight and nine of the new publication, however, were identical in matter with numbers eight and nine of the old, although published nearly two months later.

The second *Weekly Memorials*, it seems, was set up by the author, who had quarreled with Faithorne, and attempted to issue the serial himself for Chiswell, Crook and Crouch. Although the rival appears quite as well written as the original publication, it maintained the bitter competition for only twenty-nine numbers, until September 25. The original *Weekly Memorials* lasted for fifty numbers, until January 15, 1683, and, so far as can be determined, is deserving of more attention from the student. The unusual warfare between these two serials, in the days of cut-throat publishing, may be read in vindictive notices, as each conductor warned the innocent readers against the wiles of the other. That the author of the original *Weekly Memorials*, who was responsible for so much trouble, proposed an advance over previous works of the same general character, and to what extent he drew from his predecessors are indicated correctly in the prefatory statement:

The bare titles of books yearly printed in our common catalogues are somewhat dry things, scarce able to raise in men that gust and appetite to learning which we may hope these brief accounts will give them. I shall not confine myself in my undertaking only to authors of our own nation, but shall likewise give accounts of most books transmitted to us from other parts: and shall transcribe from the Paris *Journal des Savans* all that I conceive will be lookt upon here as most valuable, as well in reference to accounts of books, as to other curious novelties contained therein. . . . Mr. Oldenburg in his *Philosophical Transactions* commonly gave us something from the French Journals; Mr. Hooke in the first of his *Philosophical Collections* . . . having done the like. . . .

Like the works referred to, *Weekly Memorials* quoted fully the titles of books, used occasional wood-cut illustrations,

and consider chiefly the results of continental scholar-
ship.

A new and vital element appeared in the English literary
journal when the author of the *Universal Historical Bibliotheque,* 1686, announced his intention of giving an account
of the most considerable books printed in all languages,
"wherein a short description is given of the design and
scope of almost every book; *and the quality of the author
if known.*" This takes on the aspect of periodical criticism,
and indicates the relation of the early abstract to the later
review.

James Crossley regarded Edmund Bohun, the political
writer, as the editor of this work.[2] But nothing in the
Autobiography of Bohun supports this view. Bohun merely
states that in May 1686, when much in need of money,
he was employed in writing for the *Bibliotheque.*[3] Ames's
account of it, like that of others, seems confused. Ames
called Le Clerc one of the authors, and connected "James"
Bernard with it. He also said it lasted until 1693 and ran
into 25 volumes. But Ames, like Crossley, Cross, Parkes,
the *Encyclopedia Britannica* and *Chambers' Encyclopedia,*[4]
made the mistake of not distinguishing carefully between
periodicals published in English *in* England, and several
contemporary French publications issued from Amsterdam.
The appearance of one or more of these French serials in
the lists of early English periodicals has thrown the matter into confusion, so that a short digression is necessary
at this point. It is necessary not only for the sake of clear
exposition, but also because of the work of a Huguenot,
Jean Cornand de la Crose, on later English periodicals.

[2] *Notes and Queries,* 1st series, vol. vi, 435.
[3] 1803 (Beccles p. 76). See also J. G. Ames, *The English Periodical of Morals and Manners.* Athens, O. 1904.
[4] Maurice Cross, *Selections from the Edinburgh Review,* Intro., Lon.
1833; Samuel Parkes, *Quarterly Journal of Science, Literature and the Arts,*
vol. xiii, p. 38.

Jean Cornand, or "De la Crose," as he always signed himself, was a French protestant, born in the middle of the seventeenth century. From the scanty data available, he appears to have lived near Paris until about the time of the revocation of the Edict of Nantes by Louis XIV.[5] It is possible, even likely, that he went to Holland in the great emigration of 1681. He found his way to Amsterdam, and there became associated with Jean Le Clerc, another Huguenot, who was destined to be as important a publisher of periodicals on the continent as De la Crose was in England. Alone, De la Crose edited the *Recueil de diverses pièces concernant le Quietisme et les Quietistes,* 1688, and later, in 1694, *An Historical and Geographical Description of France,* "extracted from the best authors, both ancient and modern." He collaborated with Le Clerc from March 1686, in the labor of the first nine volumes of the *Bibliothèque universelle et historique,* printed in Amsterdam, which Le Clerc continued until 1693. Several prefaces before the ninth were signed by the two authors. The tenth volume (1688) was the first in which Le Clerc's name appeared alone. This has been taken as an indication that De la Crose withdrew from the undertaking before that time. In form the *Bibliothèque universelle et historique* was small, made up much like the *Journal des Savans,* and not greatly different from several other predecessors.[6] It may be that De la Crose, while still collaborating with Le Clerc, began to publish in London the *Universal Historical Bibliotheque.* In fact, in the preface of the October number of the *Works of the Learned* (1691) he referred to an old design to translate the French *Bibliothèque,* and

---

[5] *Nouvelle Biographie Générale,* tome xxviii, 610.

[6] The most important were the *Nouvelles de la Republique des Lettres,* 1684–9, of Pierre Bayle, published in 80–100 page parts (resumed in 1699–1718, by Jacques Bernard), and the Latin *Acta Eruditorum,* 1682–1731, of Leipsic. These and other imitators of the *Journal des Savans* were largely made up of abstracts from "learned" works.

mentioned the dates 1686–7 in connection with it. De la Crose's faulty command of English makes it difficult to be sure of his exact meaning (he confused the present and past tenses), but this seems to show that he rather than Bohun was the projector of the English *Bibliotheque*. It is rendered less certain, however, by the fact that the English periodical is not a mere translation of the one in Amsterdam, in spite of Anthony à Wood's assertion to that effect, repeated by many writers, since.[7] The truth is, only the first number derives much material from the *Bibliotheque universelle et historique*. The second and third (only three were published — January, February, and March, 1687) contained translations from the *Acta Eruditorum, Journal des Savans,* and *Il Giornali de' Letterati* of Rome and Pisa, periodicals which he did not translate exactly, so he says, but "consulted brevity and the nature of the Government we live under." The source of the material was frequently indicated in marginal notes. That the first number borrowed chiefly from the Amsterdam publication may be taken to support, perhaps, rather than refute the theory that De la Crose was the author, since that material was readily accessible to him. The chief objection to this view is the anonymity of the authorship; for De la Crose usually signed all he wrote, and in fact was scornful of those writers who refused to take such responsibility.

The earlier French serial was really an annual, published in monthly parts of 120 pages each, which were bound up in volumes at the end of each three months. The English *Bibliotheque,* on the other hand, was a real monthly periodical in intention, of about 70 pages, larger and much finer in appearance. That the editor of the English serial intended to make a step forward is indicated in the Preface

[7] *Athenae Oxonienses,* ed. Bliss, iii, 219.

where he asked for the contribution of papers, and promised an account of new books printed *in England*. He also expressed his design to publish some entire pieces that were thought worthy to be known to the world, yet were too short to be printed alone. " I shall take whatever I find omitted from the English Monthly Philosophical Transactions. . . ." This Preface contains some interesting comment on the necessity of criticism at that time and the difficulty of finding it, owing to " the divided state of Christendom " — meaning, of course, by Catholic-Protestant controversy — which he further promised not to become involved in. An original feature was the double title sometimes used at the head of abstracts — the foreign language of the original title on one side and the English equivalent on the other.

There is no available authority for the statement that De la Crose broke with Le Clerc after the tenth volume of the *Bibliothèque universelle et historique* had been issued. The former referred to himself as still connected with it when the twelfth volume was published, and in 1691 he mentioned Le Clerc in a very kindly way. It is to the French serial rather than the English that he probably referred later, when he called himself " one of the two authors of the Universal and Historical Bibliotheque," although his careless translation of the name into that of the English contemporary serial has naturally added to the confusion.

Now the *Acta Eruditorum, Bibliothèque universelle et historique,* and *Nouvelles de la République des Lettres,* as well as the *Bibliothèque choisie* and *Bibliothèque ancienne et moderne* (both by Le Clerc and in some sense continuations of his earlier work) have all been included in one or another of the lists of early English periodicals, although they were issued from foreign countries and in for-

eign languages. Obviously they cannot be regarded as
English, if indeed they frequently discussed English books.
Many English periodicals, in these and the next few years,
consisted largely of abstracts from continental works.

Yet it was not alone for the sake of making De la Crose's
early work clear that so much discussion of foreign serials
has been allowed. The stated purpose of the author of
the *Universal Historical Bibliotheque* was to draw part of
his material from publications representing the scholar-
ship of Germany, France, and Italy. The enumeration of
foreign periodicals made necessary by the foregoing discussion, impresses one with the unmeasured influence other
countries were exerting upon English ventures in this field.
Each of the periodicals mentioned undoubtedly had some
effect on English publishers, and reinforced the early and
constant influence of the *Journal des Savans.*

By 1688 the interest in abstract periodicals had reached
the Scotch capital. John Cockburn of Edinburgh was the
author in January of that year of a spirited enterprise for
a monthly serial, the *Bibliotheca Universalis,* " an historical accompt of books and transactions of the learned world."
That it was the earliest work of such a nature in Scot-
land, is now generally agreed. It was a duodecimo of 128
pages, longer than any English serial heretofore, and was
designed to be sold for sevenpence. But the first number
was the only one. Cockburn's license from the Privy Council was recalled by the Chancellor, because of passages
which gave offense to the Roman Catholics, then tolerated
by the King's proclamation. The single number of this
periodical is very rare. Its purpose and the pretentious
beginning it made give it a claim to attention.

Still another *Weekly Memorials* (this seems to have been
a popular title) began January 19, 1688, " an account of
books lately set forth, with other accounts relating to

learning." In spite of the title, the two numbers available are dated Wednesday and Saturday of the same week. This periodical is notable as the first — and probably the last — to devote each of its numbers entirely to an abstract of one book. In the first number, the author pointed out the advantages of his method, the easy access it gave to the wisdom to be found in long treatises. What would take days to read was here made accessible to the busy reader (in a single folio half-sheet). At the end of each abstract, the author employed a new device — an announcement of the contents of the following number — used by De la Crose and Dunton thereafter.

Another two-page folio half-sheet, the *Mercurius Eruditorum,* August 5, 1691, is even more interesting, as an anticipation of later forms. In a sense it was a genuine offspring of the *Term Catalogue, Philosophical Transactions,* and the early half-sheet of party propaganda. Its purpose was a discussion of books and authors, presented in dialogue form. The running title was "News from the Learned World." Beneath this, at the head of the page, was a brief synopsis of the contents, followed by the names "Alexis, Philemon, Theodore" — *dramatis personae.* The design of the work, as spoken in the first dialogue, was this: each speaker should give the others at the time of meeting, supposedly Tuesday, an account of the books he had read. They would then discuss them and "sift not only the authors of books but their journalists themselves" — meaning, apparently, the editors of other journals. They planned to select for such critical discussion only "what is most remarkable for Beauty or Defects in what comes out."

Several points especially recommend the *Mercurius Eruditorum* to notice. Successive numbers, which followed the plan outlined, contained some excellent general observa-

tions about books as well as favorable comment on such
well-known works as Wood's *Athenae Oxonienses* and
Robert Boyle's "new book of experiments." In addition,
the club or "society of gentlemen" idea was very clearly
anticipated — the idea which developed into the Spectator
Club of Addison and Steele, and much later into the Noctes
Ambrosianae of Blackwood's.

Meanwhile, the general and increasing desire for knowledge remarked around 1690 developed another form, which
is related to the serious periodicals already considered.
John Dunton, the pious and eccentric bookseller of the
Black Raven in Princes Street, began to disseminate miscellaneous information in a much more popular way than
his contemporaries, by means of a question and answer
paper called the *Athenian Gazette.* The first rude hint
of it, so he tells us in his *Life and Errors,*[8] was the idea of
"concealing the querist and answering the question." Perhaps he was unconsciously led to it by the dialogue form
of many early political papers. The result was the real
progenitor of the modern *Notes and Queries,* although not
like it in every point.

It has, however, a greater importance than that in the
history of literary periodicals. Dunton's *Athenian Gazette*
or *Casuistical Mercury,* "resolving the nice and curious
questions proposed by the Ingenious,"[9] was begun March
17, 1691. The author was soon "obliged by authority"

[8] *Life and Errors of John Dunton,* Lon. 1818, i, 189.

[9] Gildon, in his *History of the Athenian Society,* later pointed out a
remote predecessor in the *Sphinx Theologica Philosophica,* 1636 (Can-
tabrigiae).

The "Athenian" was derived from *Acts* xvii, 21, according to Dunton.
It is well to note, however, a passage in the *Mercurius Bifrons,* No. 1,
1681: "People of late have all turned Athenians, and there is much in-
quiry after news." In fact, John Taylor's pamphlet, *A Letter Sent from
London,* contains the word used in this sense as early as 1643. Probably the term was commonly thus used in Dunton's day.

(see No. 12) to change his title; so it became thereafter the *Athenian Mercury,* under which name it appeared until February, 1696.

Richard Sault, a teacher of mathematics, and Dunton were, for one number, the entire staff of the little periodical. They were soon overwhelmed with correspondence, for the ingenious were curious beyond their wildest expectations. Sault procured the aid of John Norris, who gave his services gratis, wishing apparently to assume no responsibility. After the second number had appeared, Samuel Wesley, a Church of England divine and small poet, and father of the famous John and Charles Wesley, became a partner in the undertaking. On the tenth of April Dunton, Sault, and Wesley signed articles of agreement by which the first was to have perfect editorial freedom. Sault and Wesley were to be paid ten pounds a week for a regular amount of material. They also agreed to meet Dunton regularly one day a week for consultation — over knotty questions, we may suppose.[10]

By the founders, it was regarded as of no small importance to the success of the *Mercury* that the " Intelligences " who dispensed wisdom were unknown to readers. The impression seems to have been general that a considerable group composed the " Athenian Society." But it is probable that Dunton and his three helpers constituted the staff, and — for the first year or two — answered all the questions. The editor's general knowledge, Sault's mathematics, Wesley's extensive literary and theological training, and Dr. Norris's wide reading and remarkable memory making " Athens " equal to almost any query that came in. The task they undertook seems today appalling. Like Bacon, these men took all knowledge to be their province. Consequently, the answers are sometimes little better than

10 Rawlinson MSS. vol. 72, no. 65. Bodleian Library.

evasions. Others are absurd to modern readers, just as the
questions which drew them are absurd. But humor and
common sense often saved them. Dunton and his col-
leagues, when faced with much of the superstition and
false-science of the period had a way of rationalizing, illustrated by the following:

Ques.   Why rats, toads, ravens, screech-owls, etc., are ominous,
and how they come to foreknow fatal events?

Ans.   If the querist had said unlucky instead of *ominous,* he
might easily have met with satisfaction. A rat is so
because he destroys good Cheshire cheese, and makes
dreadful ravages on a good flitch of bacon. A toad is
unlucky because it is poisonous. As for ravens, and
screech-owls, they are just as unlucky as cats, when
about their courtship, because they make an ugly noise
which disturbs the neighborhood. The instinct of rats
leaving an old ship, is because they cannot be dry in it,
an old house because they want victuals. A raven is
such a prophet as our almanack makers, foretelling
things after they are come to pass. . . . They follow
armies for the dead men, dogs, and horses that must be
left behind. . . .

Ques.   When had angels their first existence?
Ans.   Who but an angel knows?

Ques.   Whether a public or private courtship is better?
Ans.   The private is more safe and pleasant.

Occasional queries indicated a desire for guidance in matters literary. "Which is the best poem ever made?" asks
one reader. The reply considers "Grandsire" Chaucer,
"Father Ben," Shakespeare, Spenser, Davenant, and Cowley. The replier expressed the opinions that Milton's *Paradise Lost* would never be equalled, and that Waller was
the most correct poet.

Too often the Athenian Society was obliged to answer
such queries as these:

Where is the likliest place to get a husband in? Whether virtue does not consist in intention? Whether Adam was a giant? Whether negroes shall rise at the last day? Where extinguished fire goes? Whither went the ten tribes?

Aristotle and Holy Writ frequently helped out the answerers of such questions, and many a querist was referred to these two authorities. Nevertheless, the members of the Athenian Society were often compelled to exercise the utmost ingenuity in order to satisfy readers. The pressure under which they worked and the range of their investigations are indicated by a note like this, which appeared at the end of the 15th number: " The Ladies pleasant question about fleas, etc., shall be answered as soon as we have opportunity to make experiments necessary to decide the doubt proposed."

Much of the substance of the questions and answers is interesting, not from the standpoint of fact, but rather as an index to the interests of English readers at this time. For example, many questions are asked and answers given regarding the contemporary trials of witches in New England. This apparently led Dunton to sell the work of Cotton Mather on the subject, and to advertise it in the *Mercury* for many issues.[11] Other subjects very common are the nature of the soul, future life, the origin of sin, matters of love, marriage, popular superstitions, and the more mysterious phenomena of the external world.

The *Athenian Mercury* consisted of a single half-sheet folio, published, after No. 3, on Tuesdays and Saturdays. Discontinued on February 1, 1696, after 570 numbers and five supplements had been issued, it was resumed on May

---

[11] *The Wonders of the Invisible World, being an Account of the Tryals of Several Witches Lately Executed in New England. . . .* Reprinted by Dunton in London, 1693.

14, 1697, for ten numbers more. Its popularity may be judged by the fact that the great Marquis of Halifax read it — as Dunton proudly tells us in his *Life and Errors* — while Poet Laureate Tate, Peter Motteux, Defoe, Charles Richardson, and Swift sent the proprietor laudatory poems. Sir William Temple wrote frequent inquiries, and Sir Thomas Blount, Sir William Hedges, and Sir Peter Pratt commended it highly to the author.

Surprise has been expressed that Swift, especially, should have shown an extraordinary respect for the " great unknown and far-exalted " men whom he celebrated in the Pindaric ode he contributed to the *Mercury* in 1691. The same attitude is revealed in the *History of the Athenian Society,* written by Charles Gildon. Although Nichols and a few later authorities have referred to both these productions as satires, the modern student cannot dismiss them in this way. There is really nothing in either to justify such a term. To the minds of Temple, Swift, and their contemporaries, the members of the Athenian Society had accomplished a marvellous work. They had popularized knowledge and made it accessible to the mass of readers, without the poring over of dusty books. They had invented a short-cut to general education, an easy and pleasant means of satisfying the intellectual curiosity of the day.[12]

[12] A careful reading of the *History of the Athenian Society* and the prefixed poems leads me to include this note, chiefly for the sake of supporting what has already been said regarding the public reception of the *Athenian Mercury*. In the first place, the *History* was printed for James Dowley, which indicates that Dunton had at this time no hand in it. It is undated, but probably appeared about 1693, when the influence of the *Mercury* was at its height. It sold for a shilling, in its original pamphlet form.

One can easily conceive of a man like Gildon taking advantage of the popularity of the *Mercury,* and issuing what purported to be a history of the " Society," as " by a gentleman who got secret intelligence of their whole proceedings." It is even possible that Dunton was the in-

However absurd the *Athenian Mercury* may appear to readers of our day, there can be no question about its importance in the years 1691–96. Dunton's purpose to have it " lye for common chat and entertainment in every coffee-house board," was probably realized at nearly all the institutions of such nature in London. The large numbers of querists (questions were submitted in Dutch, French, Spanish, Italian, and other continental languages) and readers, the wide range of subjects appealing to all classes

---

stigator of Gildon. The public would naturally be interested to know about the mysterious source of so much wisdom.

The " Dedication " to the Society may certainly be taken seriously, as it was by Dunton. It is signed by " R. L., Your admirer and humble servant." Nothing in the prefixed verses suggests humor, much less satire. These poems, like Swift's earlier *Ode*, seem nothing less than genuine tributes, based upon the ideas that (1) the Society had given the world an easy way to universal knowledge, and (2) that it had thus conferred an unprecedented benefit upon mankind. So also, Gildon appears at all points serious in his extravagant appraisal of the Society and its work. Only now and then does a passage make the modern reader ask " Is this writer making fun of his subject? " For example, after tracing the rise of the learning through the ages, emphasizing especially the tendency of the medieval scholars to devote themselves to a few chosen disciples, Gildon declares, " All the endeavors of all the great men of all ages have not contributed so much to the increase of knowledge as the Athenian Society." Absurd? But may Gildon not have seriously meant the increase of knowledge generally among the mass of the people? Gildon mentioned the rational trend of the answers, which has already been noted, the undeceiving of readers regarding many superstitions, astrology, etc. He quotes many questions and answers, hardly one of which seems chosen for the sake of deriding the answerers. It is only a very exceptional quotation, like the question and answer on " Individuation " that leads one to suspect Gildon of writing with his tongue in his cheek. But if this is satire, it is very subtle indeed.

The most reasonable theory seems to be that Gildon, interested in getting out a book that should have a large sale, wrote what he intended to have appear a serious history of the Society, and got his friends to contribute the encomiastic verses, If he could not resist the temptation to be subtly sarcastic now and then, that is quite another matter. The History was not accepted as a satire, at any rate, or Dunton would never have referred to it as he did in his *Life and Errors*. Moreover, it was bound up with the 12th volume of the *Mercury* in 1694, and was published with his supplement of the *Athenian Oracle* in 1710.

of society, the semi-weekly frequency with which it made its appearance for five years — a long time for a periodical in those days — the honest tributes of imitators, as well as the high regard in which it seems to have been held by contemporaries: all these combine to give it an important place among the serials of this time.   Incidentally, the *Athenian Mercury* contained much verse; and because of its serious nature and its popularity did much to help break down the seventeenth-century feeling that poetry was always somehow associated with flippancy and vice — a feeling expressed by De la Crose, about this time.   Gildon, in his *History,* showed how the *Mercury* had revealed poetry to be a medium for virtuous and serious thought.

If there are any predecessors of this question and answer periodical, they have not been discovered.   But a score of other publishers, in the two decades which followed, were glad to employ in some form Dunton's popular device to engage the reading public.   Even Defoe's *Review* and the *Gentleman's Magazine* were the debtors of the *Athenian Mercury* in this particular — alone enough to give Dunton's serial an assured place in the history of English literary periodicals.[13]

The *Athenian Mercury* continued to scatter abroad its miscellaneous information until February 8, 1696, when the publisher announced that owing to " the glut of news, the coffee-houses having the votes every day, and six newspapers every week," he had determined to drop the weekly edition, and would continue the design in volumes.   Revived for a few numbers in 1697, as has been seen, the

---

[13] " By the Athenian Society " became a kind of trade name for Dunton, the publisher and bookseller.   The *Athenian Library,* the *Athenian Oracles* in various editions, the *Young Students Library,* 1692, a translation of Lucian, 1695, and *Athenian Sport,* 1707, were all advertised and sold by him, as " By the Athenian Society " or " 'By a member of the Athenian Society."

Athenian Mercury soon ceased publication for good and all. Dunton's plan for a monthly periodical called the *Oracle* had to be abandoned, but the popularity of Athenian wisdom seems to have continued. In 1703, a selection of the best questions and answers in the old *Mercuries,* appeared with the title *Athenian Oracle.* It was signed " Edw. Smith, a member of the Athenian Society." A second edition in three volumes was put out in 1704, signed " S. W." (Samuel Wesley). The third edition in 1728 consisted of four volumes. In 1820, an abridged edition was published, and the publisher of Scott's Library issued a volume of selections in 1892.

A Supplement to the Athenian Oracle, 1710, has been called spurious, inasmuch as Gildon's *History* and the poetical tributes quoted were prefixed. But the questions and answers do not appear different from those in the other *Oracles.* This *Supplement* was printed for Andrew Bell, who at this time owned the rights of the *Athenian Oracle.*[14] It is worth noting, also, that in the questions and answers Dunton's old controversy with the Anabaptists is continued. There seems to be no reason for disagreeing with the editor of the *Term Catalogue,* who assigns it to Dunton.

Dunton's relations with Defoe deserve a word at this point. The latter contributed to the *Mercury,* and wrote for Dunton an essay on the bookseller's father-in-law, " the Character of Dr. Annesley," which Defoe later reprinted as his own property, causing Dunton much discomfiture.[15] But the chief connecting link is suggested in Dunton's reference to Defoe's " clogging " his question-project, meaning, of course, by his " Advice from the Scandalous Club " in the *Review,* its supplements, and the *Little Review* (1705). Dunton complained that Defoe's answering ques-

[14] See Rawlinson MSS. vol. 72. No. 67. [15] *Life and Errors,* ii. 432.

tions weekly put a stop to his own plan for a monthly *Oracle*, "for though his answers were false and impertinent . . . yet being published every Tuesday, they ruined my Monthly Oracle; for most are seized with the Athenian Itch and chuse rather to be scratched weekly than stay till the month is out for a perfect cure." It is profitless to recount the bickerings and egotistical complaints of Dunton against Defoe. But his really high regard for the greatest journalist of that day is worth remark. Although he challenged him with questions of grammar, Dunton admitted Defoe to be " a very ingenious, useful Writer," and a man of courage. Their later relations seem to have been amicable, for the Bodleian Library contains articles of agreement between them for the publication of a paper, to be called the *Hanover Spy*.[16]

As has been intimated, the remarkable success of the *Athenian Mercury* did not go long unchallenged. On February 1, 1692, Tom Brown — school teacher, miscellaneous writer, and "merry wag about town " — set up his *London Mercury* on similar lines (with No. 9, the title was changed to *Lacedemonian Mercury*). One Pate was Brown's partner in this " aping " undertaking, so Dunton tells us. The proprietor of the *Athenian Mercury* met the competition with firmness and dispatch. He advertised that all questions answered in Brown's paper should be answered again in his own — " with amendments." In addition, the life of Brown was to be " exposed." The threat of the last was evidently effective, for we are informed that the two staffs met at the Three Cranes, and under some pressure Brown agreed to stop his paper. The last issue was on May 28.

---

[16] Rawlinson MSS. vol. 72, No. 49. A rough draft on the back of a letter to Dunton from his daughter. The agreement is dated October 28, 1717.

Another short-lived imitator was the *Jovial Mercury* of
1693. The few copies available show that it was a weekly,
begun on March 3. It is distinguished by the fact that it
employed the question and answer as a vehicle for amusement, since the *Athenian Mercury* — it has been noted —
was primarily a serious publication. " Whether women
have rational souls? Whether at the skip of a flea the
earth moves out of its center? Whether poets, musicians,
and painters are half-crackt? " Such queries indicate the
humorous trend. Although its purpose was primarily entertainment, the *Jovial Mercury* was not entirely devoted
to such material. Several " characters " were included,
and in the last two numbers were moral paradoxes — " An
Atheist, if not a fool, is the most pernicious creature in the
world," and " Duelling, a kind of Madness " — showing an
interest in the reform of manners and morals.

A few numbers, likewise, are all that we have of the
Ladies Mercury (beginning February 28, 1694) a semi-
weekly half-sheet folio, differing at this time from the
Athenian Mercury only in the length of the questions, of
which there were sometimes only three or four in the two
pages. The tendency to longer questions and answers may
be seen, however, in the later numbers of Dunton's periodical. It is significant, for it led directly to the letters of correspondents answered by Steele in the *Tatler*. The name,
Ladies Mercury, was a misnomer, for gentlemen as well as
ladies were " desired " to send their questions relating to
love to the Latin Coffee-House. The author appears to
have been the pioneer in advice to the lovelorn.

The *Athenian Mercury* and its imitators represent at-
tempts to satisfy in a popular way the general desire for
knowledge. While such serials were dispensing information in palatable form, the " learned " periodical was continuing its unbroken line of progress, under the energetic

De la Crose. The Huguenot proposed in his *History of Learning* (July 1691) to give English readers of foreign journals an abstract serial of their own, treating new works at home as well as abroad, but (and this is a characteristic of De la Crose's work from the first to last) considering only such works as deserved the perusal of the studious and serious reader.[17] He asked in the preface of the first number to be excused from giving critical judgments, yet by his proposed plan actually assumed the office of censor. With a characteristic lack of humor, he writes:

The reader must excuse me, if I omit giving a Judgment upon the style and language of authors; which I shall avoid, and chuse rather to give an account of things than words. I shall also, as little as possible, take any side in the disputes of learned men; or if it should happen that I adhere to one party in such disputes, I hope the ingenious reader will believe it to be the force of reason and truth that draws me to its side.

De la Crose exhibited further inconsistency by promising to "mark out the most considerable passages, and the places best writ of every author." And he did this marking by comment and the occasional use of italics. Here are surely the beginnings of literary criticism. Saintsbury declared this work of De la Crose's to be the first deserving of the name "literary periodical."[18] It must be agreed that the articles it contained were real reviews in almost every point.

[17] The idea of such a work as the title implies is an old one. It has been traced to Apollodorus of Athens, 240 B.C., and Diodorus of Sicily, in the reign of Augustus. But the student of periodicals need go no further back than the *Journal des Savans* to find De la Crose's inspiration.

[18] *Chambers' Encyclopedia* states that the beginnings of the literary periodicals are to be found in the pamphlets of the 17th century; Crossley named the *Philosophical Transactions* first; Andrews (*British Journalism*) called the *Mercurius Librarius* first; Parkes and Nichols found *Weekly Memorials* deserving of the title; Ames made out a case for the *Athenian Mercury;* all of which shows how profitless is the search for the "first."

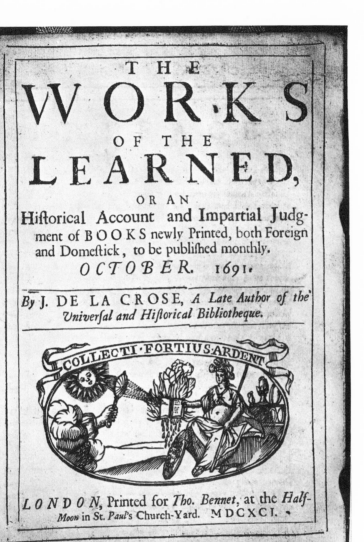

THE
WORKS
OF THE
LEARNED,

OR AN

Hiſtorical Account and Impartial Judgment of BOOKS newly Printed, both Foreign and Domeſtick, to be publiſhed monthly.

OCTOBER. 1691.

By J. DE LA CROSE, *A Late Author of the Vniverſal and Hiſtorical Bibliotheque.*

COLLECTI·FORTIUS·ARDENT

LONDON, Printed for *Tho. Bennet,* at the *Half-Moon* in St. *Paul's* Church-Yard. MDCXCI.

A LITTLE-KNOWN ANCESTOR OF THE MODERN REVIEW

The *History of Learning* began with the July number. The public response was a disappointment to the projector, as he intimates in a later preface, laying the blame on the bookseller with whom he was engaged. A change of booksellers was one result, therefore. Another was the appearance in August of, not a second number but an entirely new periodical, the *Works of the Learned,* which was continued until February, 1692. For convenience, we shall consider the two periodicals as one, for only very slight changes were apparent in the form and plan of the second. A catalogue of books for the following month was added, and at the end, in later numbers, a department entitled " the News of Learning," which was broken into items from France, Italy, Holland, and other countries, after the manner of Bayle's *Nouvelles de la République des Lettres* of 1684. In some degree, the author intended his new work to take the place of the *Philosophical Transactions,* which he thought about to be given up. This is one reason why so many of the 64 pages of the first number are taken up with scientific discussions.

As has been noted, the articles in the *History of Learning* and the *Works of the Learned,* although mainly composed of abstract or translation, approach later reviews in character in that they do contain an element of criticism, however simple it may seem when compared with critiques of a century later. The most interesting to the modern reader are those in which L'Estrange's *Fables,* Raleigh's *Arts of Empire,* Sir William Temple's *Memoirs,* and Wood's *Athenae Oxonienses* are treated. Too many of the articles, however, have to do with such topics as a " Project of a Method for the Reform of Men's Morals," a " Defense of Pluralities," or " A New Explication of the Deluge." De la Crose explains, perhaps, why this is so when he indicates his moral purpose. He declared he could not mention works of light nature, "plays, satyrs, Romances, and the like," since they were "fitter to corrupt men's morals, and to shake the grounds of natural religion, than to promote learning and piety." That De la Crose had such a feeling, helps us to understand the later corrective efforts of Defoe and Steele.

The relations between Dunton and De la Crose are important in the history of literary periodicals, and the articles signed by Dunton, Sault and Wesley in April, 1691, bore upon these relations in a peculiar way. The last item in these articles was an agreement that Dunton should get translated by other hands the *Acta Eruditorum,* the *Journal des Savans, Bibliothèque universelle et historique,* and *Giornale de 'Letterati,* or any other periodicals, and add to the *Athenian Mercury* as many numbers as he pleased, thus invading the proper field of the " learned " periodicals already discussed. Accordingly the first volume of the *Mercury* was closed with the thirtieth number, and the first supplement issued. This was in May, 1691. It will be remembered that De la Crose's *History of Learning* did not appear until July. Dunton's later reference to this periodical as based upon an idea of his own has been regarded lightly. But these facts show that there was justice in his assertion. For the first as well as later supplements of the *Mercury* were made up entirely of just such material as De la Crose later used in the *History* — abstracts of books translated from foreign periodicals — and in addition, translated excerpts from " A new book entitled *Entretiens sérieuses et galantes* " — a book of questions and answers.

The preface to the fourth declared, " These Supplements will be continued constantly by several learned persons, and comprehend a brief idea of all the valuable books published from time to time; " but in the fifth (January 30, 1692) Dunton announced a change. Henceforth, he designed to make the supplements a kind of natural history of England and other countries, containing all sorts of information — from the kinds of fishes to celestial phenomena, or from remarkable crimes to local happenings. He here mentioned De la Crose's useful design, which he declared his *Supplement* would not in the future supplant. The explanation of Dunton's change of heart is simple. He had become financially interested in De la Crose's work, which was licensed for him and registered by the Stationer's Company on February 22, 1692, although the Huguenot remained editor of it until it was stopped. Accordingly, in the preface to the sixth volume of the *Athenian Mercury* (no supplements appeared after the fifth) Dunton advertised that he had bought the rights of the *Works of the Learned,* which would now be carried on " by a London Divine." Nevertheless the last issue of this serial, consisting of March and April numbers in one, bore De la Crose's name.

In May appeared a virtual continuation of it, the *Compleat Library or News for the Ingenious,* printed monthly for John Dunton and conducted by him, although R. Wooley was named as editor. Its nine sheets (36 pages) Dunton planned to divide thus: three for original pieces, four for historical accounts of books in England and in foreign journals, two for " notes on memorable passages happening monthly, as well as the state of learning in the world." Although this original plan of contents was followed pretty well up to May, 1693, after that the monthly became a quarterly, and consisted only of a long catalogue of books, and a short section of news, " from the learned world." It was stopped in April, 1694. The original articles, while they lasted, were invariably concerned with matters of scriptural interpretation and controversy, and have little relation to literature. The reviews of the catalogue, on the other hand, furnished further interesting illustrations of the near approach to reviews of a later day. Some of them, of course, were very short. But others ran to a length of five or six pages. The *Reformed Gentleman* called forth a page of discussion of morals in general, then two pages of comment on and quotations of the preface, explaining the character and purpose of the work, and finally, a three-page epitome of its contents. Shear's *Polybius,* Volume I, was excuse for an account of the historian's life, his fitness to write history, and his influence. Matters of "stile" were not beyond the scope of the *Compleat Library,* as reviews of Blount's *De re Poetica* and Rymer's *Short View of Tragedy* demonstrate.

In *Memoirs for the Ingenious* (January — December, 1693) De la Crose continued the progress of the serious type of periodical with which his name will always be associated. The author signed himself, in this case, " J. De la Crose, E. A. P." The new form indicated in the sub-heading, "In Miscellaneous Letters," showed that De la Crose was not uninfluenced by the less serious *Gentleman's Journal* of Motteux, which had been started the preceding year. Each number of the 32-page monthly *Memoirs* consisted of letters, written to eminent scholars of the day like Sir Robert Southwell, President of the Royal Society, or Richard Sault, the mathematician, or Dr. Samuel Garth, the famous physician. Again, as in the *Works of the Learned,* De la Crose remarked that few papers of the Royal Society had appeared since Oldenburg's death. The *Memoirs* were to take the place of the *Transactions,* in some degree, and to contain " all that is new and short and rare, and may make men more learned and good." Such subjects as the origin of fountains, the shape of the earth, experiments with lodestone, and theories of " petrification," filled its columns.

De la Crose's serial appeared for only one full year, but a follower seems to have had a career of only one number. *Memoirs for the Ingenious,* or "the Universal Mercury" (January 1694) was designed as a monthly of the same type, except that the "several hands" who professed to conduct it made an effort to popularize their erudition. The authors imitated De la Crose in attempting to convey their learning in letters . . . "whatever is curious in all sorts of learning . . . not contrary to religion, good manners, or government." The announcement of contents included "Philology and all its known criticisms" — a fact worth noting. The six letters of the single number show the effort made by the authors to avoid raw and undigested ideas, as they put it in the preface, and to present information in a form more acceptable to the reader.

The letter form must have had a strong appeal, for the second *Memoirs for the Ingenious* was followed immediately by *Miscellaneous Letters,* a weekly serial of the same type, during the closing months of 1694. In January, 1695, it became a monthly serial, continuing in this form until March, 1696, with a total of 25 numbers. Historically, the *Miscellaneous Letters* is distinguished as the first serious English periodical to contain discussion of the stage. Although in letter form, and only as translations from the French, yet the long *Dissertation* in condemnation of the stage and players (No. 10) and the *Refutation* (No. 11) represent new material for this sort of publication. Furthermore, we find in No. 12 a review-abstract of Plutarch's *Lives,* and in No. 13 another on De Corneille's French *Dictionary of the Arts and Sciences,* while earlier numbers, of interest to the modern student, contain articles on Wotton's *Reflections on Ancient and Modern Learning,* and Sir William Temple's *Introduction to the History of England.*

Another *History of Learning* appeared in May, 1694, a

feeble imitation of De la Crose's earlier work. It was a quarto, licensed by D. Poplar. Only one number survives, and it seems unlikely that more were published, for this contains only a long abstract of the *Memoires* of Frederic Maurice, a translation of a review from the *Histoire des Ouvrages des Savans* (a follower of the *Journal des Savans*), and extracts of letters, also translated from the *Ouvrages*.

There is reason to believe the last years of De la Crose's life were spent in labor upon a *History of the Works of the Learned*, or "an impartial account of books printed in all parts of Europe, with a particular relation to the state of learning in each country." It was issued from January 1699 to 1711, as a 60-page monthly serial. The title page bore the cryptic "done by several hands." Conducted on the same general plan as the *Works of the Learned* of 1691, its reviews were fuller, and the contributed articles were sometimes as long as 16 pages. Good examples of reviews are the articles on Collier's *Second Defence of the Short View, etc.* (January 1700) and the *Privileges of the House of Commons* (October 1701). Like the earlier serials of De la Crose, this one avoided the "trifling" books — did not even mention their titles (see introduction to No. 1). The authors designed to hold the middle course "between tedious extracts and superficial catalogues made up only of title and preface, the former being tiresome to the reader as well as injurious to the sale of books; and the latter being a mere imposition on the Publick." According to his biographer, George Ridpath, a well known journalist of the day, "assisted" on the staff of the periodical, although there is probably no reason for calling him editor.

The first number of the *History of the Works of the Learned* was reprinted in April, 1699, by James Watson of Edinburgh, and sold to readers for sevenpence, a lower price than it brought in London. His promise to continue the publication of a Scottish edition was kept for eight numbers at least. Those are all that can now be found.

James Baldwin, a London publisher, had brought out in 1701 another *Memoirs for the Curious*, "an account of that which is Rare, Secret, Extraordinary, Prodigious, or Miraculous . . . in Nature, Art, Learning, Policy, or Religion." It was conducted by means of a "settled correspondence" with most known parts of the world. This monthly serial is especially interesting as an example of the effort to satisfy public interest in the strange and curious — an effort that connects it with the earlier *Athenian Mercury* and the later miscellany form, although the table of contents would hardly remind one of the *Gentleman's Magazine* or *Blackwood's*. As a matter of fact, it was an unsuccessful attempt to turn the "learned" periodical into one of entertainment. But such subjects as "a Dutch Child having Hebrew and Latin characters about the pupils of its eyes," "Thoughts of an Indian heathen," or "a Serpent Found in the Heart of a Man" (illustrated) were evidently not calculated to give it long popularity.

Many of the periodicals that followed included the question and answer among other features, but the best later example of the type was undoubtedly the *British Apollo* (1708-1711) "Performed by a Society of Gentlemen." A four-page folio, published on Wednesdays and Fridays until No. 79, and then thrice a week, for a total of 410 issues, it differed from the earlier *Athenian Mercury* in containing much more verse — not always decent — exchange and treasury reports, and "the most material occurrences, foreign and domestic." It differed also in the undisguised obscenity of many of the questions and answers, inasmuch as the "Athenians" had always consistently refused to answer such inquiries. On the other hand, one finds similarity in the pious cant of other questions and those of Dunton's serial. As in the *Ladies Mercury,* questions or answers were often so long as to approach closely the letters of the *Tatler.* They covered a very wide range — from mathematics to gallantry and theology — and became so numerous that twenty-one 12-page monthly supplements and five 12-page quarterly supplements were issued. The news space diminished, as time passed, and the quality of the verse could hardly permit it to have a wide appeal; so the explanation of the *British Apollo's* success must be laid partly to the " noble " subscribers, who subsidized the publication, and partly to the questions and answers. In March, 1710, it was announced that the *Apollo* would henceforth be published independent of said subscribers, and would take its place in the world like any other periodical. The independence was enjoyed for a year, until the serial became defunct in May, 1711.

That the youthful Aaron Hill was a contributor to the *Apollo,* is established by the fact that a dozen or more of his poems, unsigned, appear in the early numbers. A list of these poems, which appear also in Hill's acknowledged works, is to be found in Dorothy Brewster's *Aaron Hill.*[19] Hill later became, with William Bond, a notable author of the *Plain Dealer,* one of the best of the followers of the *Spectator.*

Competition may have been the chief cause of the discontinuance of the *British Apollo.* Dunton had entered the field on March 7, 1710, with his *Athenian News, or Dunton's Oracle,* a four-page, twice-a-week paper, largely consisting of questions and answers. It was avowedly antagonistic to the *British Apollo,* which Dunton called " dull, ignorant, and stupid." It ran for twenty-seven numbers, until June 6, satirizing the *British Apollo* whenever it was

---

[19] See Dorothy Brewster, *Aaron Hill,* N. Y. 1913. p. 18.

possible, and copying certain features of the *Tatler,* among them the long letter or essay at the beginning. One department was called regularly the " Casuistical Post, or Athenian Mercury," another made up of sappy letters, the " Love-Post " or the " Sibil-Post." Occasional departments were also a " Miser's Post " and a " Rhiming Post " — the latter containing several columns of verse.

In the preceding pages, an effort has been made to trace, with some chronological coherence, the development of what may be termed the " learned " periodical, the obvious response to the demand for information on all sorts of subjects. Advertisements, book catalogues, and abstract-serials imitated from the French, all play a part in the evolutionary process. The jog-trot summaries of earliest serials became the abstract-reviews of 1700. Such development has involved the beginnings of criticism in periodicals and the impulse to reform, although neither is limited to the serious type of publication we have been discussing, but is to be found quite as frequently in periodicals of entertainment.

II

THE PERIODICAL OF AMUSEMENT

THE effort to furnish entertainment in serial form brought a considerable change in the character of periodicals in the second half of the seventeenth century. The seeds were sown far back in the pamphlets and corantos, in the bitterly personal satire and ribald jests of political controversialists. The derisive tone of many small political half-sheets easily developed a form of serial, published for the sole purpose of amusing. There were, moreover, popular amusing tracts such as the *French Mountbank* (1643) and the pamphlets of John Taylor and his contemporaries. In fact, the *Harleian Miscellany* contains tracts dated as far back as 1608 which might be cited. [1] The effort to gain and hold the attention of readers by amusing them led one step further to the issuing of such serials as the *Mercurius Fumigosus, News from Hell, Mercurius Melancholicus, Mercurius Morbicus, Mercurius Medicus,* and *Mercurius Elencticus* of 1647, and later, to the *Man in the Moon,* 1649, *Mercurius Democritus,* and *Mercurius Phreneticus,* 1652, as well as the *Mercurius Jocosus* of 1654. Written in a swaggering style, often containing scraps of Rabelaisian verse, full of pointed and obscene personal allusions, and of savage, morbid humor — these news and political sheets are hard to classify. It is difficult to tell when and to what extent the author endeavors to entertain his readers. There is entertainment in them even to-

[1] See the *Pennyless Parliament of Thread-bare Poets; or, All Mirth and Witty Conceits — Harleian Miscellany.* Vol. I. 180.

day, but one can never be sure the authors intended them primarily for amusement.

By 1680, however, it is evident that authors have discovered a reading public for papers with little or no party or cause. *News from Parnassus* (from No. 2 called *Advice from Parnassus*) which began February 2, 1680, gave the proceedings of the " Grand Council of Virtuoso and Literati," in a highly allegorical treatment of social and political affairs, written in a sort of burlesque of the *Sueños* of Quevedo, which L'Estrange had translated thirteen years before. *The Strange and Wonderful News from Norwich,* a few months later, is another representative of a class of serials in which the modern reader can discern little propaganda. *Heraclitus Ridens, or a discourse between Jest and Earnest* (1681), an authorized comic weekly, represents what may be called the politico-comic periodical. The *Weekly Discovery, Weekly Discoverer Stripp't Naked, Democritus Ridens, Mercurius Infernus, Mercurius Bifrons,* and *News from the Land of Chivalry,* in 1681, are some of the many which might be cited as examples of a transition state. The controversies, religious or political, which brought most of these small publications into being, do not concern us here. But the ribaldry, the burlesque news and mock advertisements, the fact that an effort was made by authors to attract and entertain readers as well as inform and persuade them — all point the way toward the magazine of entertainment of a later day. In this progress, books had a great influence, of course. Such early works as Winstanley's *Muses Cabinet,* 1655, or the *Sportive Wit,* or *Muses Merriment,* 1656, contain exactly the sort of entertainment that soon came to be provided in serial form. While such foreign periodicals of amusement as the *Muse Historique* (1651) of Jean Loret, exerted an influence on English publishers and authors impossible now to estimate.

This increasing effort to amuse as well as instruct or persuade may be seen also in journals like L'Estrange's *Observator* of 1681, where such sub-titles as the "Adventures of Kid the Coffee Man, Three or Four Parsons Dissected in the Pulpit, Horses to be Sainted in Baxter's Calendar," or "The Ass to the Prophet," were employed to catch the reader. Two news sheets among those cited are worth special consideration. The *Mercurius Bifrons; or the English Janus,* like the others, a single half-sheet folio, had the "True and Serious Intelligencer" on one side and the "Jocular Intelligencer" on the other. It thus devoted one half its space to "news from Heaven and Hell, from Purgatory and Elizium, From East and West, from North and South, from beyond the sea and at home, from the World of the Moon, Utopia, Parnassus, Terra Incognita, the Isle of Pines, etc." Within the same month was started the *News from the Land of Chivalry, containing the Pleasant and Delectable History of Rugero de Strangemento, Kt. of the Squeaking Fiddle,* in which such news and history were told in narrative of a highly allegorical and amusing sort.

In 1688 appeared *Poor Robin's Occurrences and Remarks,* written "for the sake of merriment and harmless recreation." The next year saw the publication of the *Rambles around the World, or the travels of Kainophilos,* a weekly folio, to which was added the *Irish Courant.* While *Momus Ridens,* 1690, in form much like the *Tatler* of Steele, contained verse along with its "comical remarks on publick reports," and sections of facetious newsmatter dated "From the Hague," "From Westminster" or "From Whitehall." All such serials, because of their evident design for entertainment (whatever their actual purpose) are in a sense remote ancestors of miscellanies and essay sheets of the eighteenth century.

This effort to amuse the reader resulted in a two-fold development, in the last decade of the seventeenth century. Two types of entertaining serials had evolved. The one is valuable for its employment of the " character " and for the light it throws on taverns and coffee-houses and manners of the period, yet is almost invariably condemned by its obsession with the ugly and obscene side of life. A progenitor of this type was the *Mercurius Fumigosus or Smoking Nocturnall* (1654), which represents a great many such serials in the Century. It began with bad verse, and its eight pages were filled with coarse amusement, never rising above a certain stupid mediocrity.

The best known and most able author of this sort of serial is Edward Ward. His *London Spy* (1698–1700) a sixteen-page folio, presented the character of a countryman guided about London by a city acquaintance, a notable anticipation, though not the only one by any means, of Sir Roger de Coverley. The *Spy* is full of well drawn sketches of London life, showing the author's keen observation. It appeared monthly, filled with much that was coarse and filthy, and much that is unintelligible patter to the present-day reader. The wit often seems clumsy and the gaiety forced. The essay form was used, however, and the author wrote from the first person point-of-view. Sometimes he was allegorical in the moral manner of Steele and Addison. Frequently he included verse in the columns of the *Spy;* and among the " characters " for which Ward is famous are those of the Quack, the Banker, and the Gossip.

Another publication of the less reputable type, likewise valuable as a precursor of the *Tatler,* was the *English Lucian* (January 18 — April 18, 1698) " or weekly discoveries of the witty intrigues, comical passages, and remarkable transactions in town and country; with reflections on the vices and vanities of the times." In its form and make-up, it closely approximated the work of Steele. It was filled with

facetious news, often lewd, dated from different places —
" White-chapel, Lincoln-Inn-Fields, Old Baly (*sic*), Drury-
Lane, Lombard Street, St. James," and " From my Lodg-
ings in Kent Street." The last two suggest the " St. James
Coffee-House " and " From My Apartment," of Steele.
In spite of its reflections on the vices and vanities of the
times, no reforming aim can be detected by the most pains-
taking reader of this half-sheet. But the dating thus of the
news from well known places anticipates the *Tatler,* and
the considerable space given to satirical comment on " Partridge John, a foreteller of things," suggests the fun that
Bickerstaff derived from abuse of the same astrologer, John
Partridge. That it was published like the *Tatler,* three
times a week, is suggestive but not important. The *English
Lucian,* printed for John Harris who had lately returned
from America, was continued for at least fifteen numbers —
that being the number in the Burney Collection at the
British Museum.

The *Weekly Comedy,* " as it is daily acted at most Coffee-
Houses in London," deserves special note because of its originality. *Dramatis personae* were announced at the head
of the title page, namely:

Snarl, *a disbanded Captain*	Squabble, *a lawyer*
Truck, *a merchant*	Whim, *a projector*
Scribble, *a newswriter*	Log, *a mariner*
All-craft, *a turncoat*	Scan-all, *a poet*
Cant, *a precision*	Plush, *a quack*
Snap, *a sharper*	Prim, *a beau*

Five of these anticipate very distantly the characters of the
notable *Spectator* group. Ned Ward is now regarded as the
author of this weekly half-sheet folio, which appeared May
10, 1699, and ran for at least ten numbers. The characters
were not all intended to speak on one occasion, but the

author used them as he saw fit. The average number of speakers in each copy was three or four. Some of the figures may be considered well delineated " characters," although in most cases traits were poorly developed. The " club " idea was suggested, but not definitely brought out.

The *Infallible Astrologer,* October 16, 1700, of one who called himself " Sylvester " Partridge, (probably another thrust at John Partridge, the butt of various periodical journalists and later of both Swift and Steele) must certainly be included in this category, for his " Prophesie and predictions of what shall infallibly happen in, and about the cities of London and Westminster," furnished a section of the reading public weekly with undisguised salacity.

Likewise, the *Merry Mercury, or a Farce of Fools,* of the same year, because of its matter, is condemned to inclusion in this group. Its form recommends it to attention, however, for the contents were presented, like those of *Momus Ridens* and the *English Lucian,* as advices dated from various well known places in and out of England — facetious and lewd advices though they were.[2]

This division of the journal into parts suggestive of the later *Tatler* is further seen in the *Secret Mercury,* September 1702, which took the form of seven " rambles " on the seven days of the week. In design, it was much like Dunton's *Night-Walker* of 1696, turned, however, to less pious uses. A table of contents which appeared at the head of each weekly number indicates only too clearly its nature: (1) The character of Madame L — of Hackney, (2) a conference with a night-walker, (3) an essay on Bedlam, (4) Remarks on the innocent adultery acted Saturday, (5) A character of the Reverend Mr. F —— d, (6) A discovery in More-fields, (7) The cheats of the cloysters. As one may

---

[2] The *Jesting Astrologer* of 1700 was likewise a faithful follower of Ned Ward, in the nature of its comment on London life.

guess from these topics, the tone of the *Secret Mercury* is extremely coarse. The periodical is noteworthy only for its form, " characters," and entertaining aim.

The *Diverting Post,* like the *Weekly Comedy,* made a slight advance in this line of development. The author, who signed himself " H. P." (undoubtedly Henry Playford, who printed and sold it) designed his weekly half-sheet folio to entertain " those only, whose understanding and judgment have been refined, by liberal education and genteel conversation, from the heavy dross which clogs the reason of the vulgar; who take delight in the pleasing paths of poetry, not in the rugged ways of business; who had rather line their heads than their pockets. . . ." He promised to publish all manuscripts sent in, provided they were free from scurrilous language and immodest reflections. After such prefatory eloquence, it is sad to recount the swift moral decline of the *Diverting Post* in its rather brief career (October 28, 1704 to June 30, 1705, as a half-sheet weekly; then during January and February, 1706, as a ten-page monthly). It began well enough, filled with occasional verse, newsmatter, and dialogues spoken by such " characters " as Mr. Blunt and Mr. Grumbleton, or Mr. Stingy and Mr. Freeman. By January, 1705, the newsmatter had disappeared as well as the dialogues. From this point on the *Diverting Post* was made up entirely of verse — prologues for Wilkes, Booth, and Betterton, riddles in verse, limericks, and long poems. Like many of its predecessors, it became, as it progressed, less and less delicate in its treatment of sex. Its ignominious end came in February, 1706.[3] Meanwhile, in January, such unpublished poems as the editor had found too elaborately indecent for the *Diverting*

---

[3] Playford's name appears again in 1699–1702. He was one of the two editors of the *Mercurius Musicus,* a twelve-page monthly folio made up of songs with music. This serial is noteworthy as the first musical journal in English, although several had used sheet music as a feature.

Post, had been issued by Samuel Philips as the weekly
Poetical Courant.[4] Many of the verses were dated from
Oxford, but that does not save the character of this disreputable sheet, which appears to have been published for
only thirty numbers.

Almost identical in design with the *Weekly Comedy* of
1699 was Ward's weekly four-page sheet of 1707. It was
headed, *The Humours of a Coffee-House,* as daily acted by

Levy, *a recruiting officer*	Querpo, *a quack*
Hazard, *a gamester*	Trick, *a lawyer*
Bite, *a sharper*	Horoscope, *an astrologer*
Nice, *a Beau*	Shuffle, *a time-server*
Blunt, *a plain dealer*	Bays, *a poet*
Whim, *a projector*	Compass, *a sailor*
Venture, *a merchant*	Harlem, *a news-writer*
Talley, *a stock jobber*	Boker, *the coffee-man*

Like its predecessor, this serial was written in dramatic dialogue, introducing several of the sixteen characters in each
number. Eight of the *dramatis personae,* it may be noted,
correspond exactly with those of the earlier publication. In
the later numbers, the title read " as it is acted by town and
country," the list of characters being omitted. It appeared
weekly, from June to December, for a total of at least 19
numbers; and was printed " for the benefit of Boker, the
Coffee-Man."

The *Wandering Spy,* a four-page octavo, 1705, and finally
Ward's own *London Terrae Filius, or Satyrical Reformer,*
1707–8, represent the logical end of this line of development toward filth and obscenity. Both were short-lived. Of
the former, only a few issues are now to be found, while the

---

[4] Although it was published anonymously, the Bodleian copy of No. 1
has, written in faded ink, " by Samuel Philips, Gent., late of St. John's
Coll., Oxon. See note to number 12." The note referred to is of such
a nature that it seems certain the annotator must have identified the
author from personal allusions in the poems.

latter appeared as a 32-page monthly for only six numbers. Some merit may be found for the *Wandering Spy* in the fact that numbers were filled with single essays, written in a narrative and allegorical style, while the reforming trend of the times is suggested by Ward's publication, however perverted the reform may appear to the student of today. It is unnecessary to discuss such periodicals further in this study. By 1709 their service in the evolution of the literary periodical had been accomplished. Ward's publications, especially, had added some impetus to the reforming tendency respecting men's manners and morals, paradoxical as it may seem. They had also helped to develop the "character," as a device for securing concreteness. But what is more important, they had given readers much entertainment in serial form, making much more urgent the necessity for amusing readers.

So much for one tendency of the effort to entertain readers in seventeenth-century periodicals. The other line of development was a healthier one and a thriftier one as well.

The best example of this before 1700 was the *Gentleman's Journal* of Peter Anthony Motteux which appeared first in January, 1692. Motteux was another Huguenot who had come to England at the revocation of the Edict of Nantes. Plays and translations give him some title to notice in this period, and he had been for several years a contributor to periodicals. Motteux was a man of letters, not a scholar nor a politician. This is important, for it means that in 1692, for the first time, the periodical of entertainment was in the hands of professional writers.

Motteux modeled his *Journal* on *Le Mercure Galant,* a sort of Town Topics of Paris, which owed its popularity to the prominence it gave court news and gossip. The French publication (1673–4 and 1678–9) was designed for the peru-

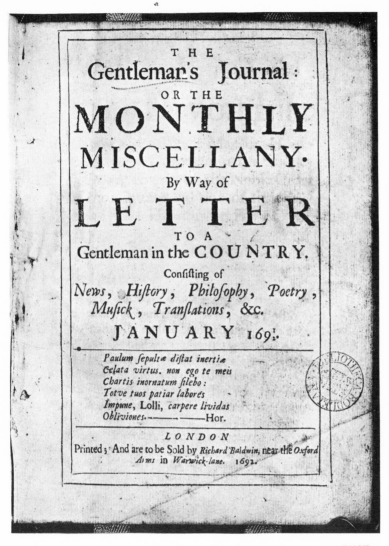

THE
Gentleman's Journal:
OR THE
MONTHLY
MISCELLANY.
By Way of
LETTER
TO A
Gentleman in the COUNTRY.
Consisting of
News, History, Philosophy, Poetry,
Musick, Translations, &c.
JANUARY 169½.

Paulum sepultæ distat inertiæ
Celata virtus. non ego te meis
Chartis inornatum silebo:
Totve tuos patiar labores
Impune, Lolli, carpere lividas
Obliviones.————————Hor.

LONDON
Printed; And are to be Sold by *Richard Baldwin*, near the *Oxford*
Arms in *Warwick-lane.* 1692.

THE *GENTLEMAN'S JOURNAL* WAS THE FIRST MAGAZINE
IN A MODERN SENSE

sal of the smart set, who made many contributions to it. Each number was in the form of a letter to a lady who had left Paris for the provinces, but wanted to keep in touch with her friends of fashion. Motteux acknowledged his considerable debt, in that he employed the letter device in his *Journal* — this time to a gentleman in the country rather than a lady.[5]

The *Gentleman's Journal* was such a miscellany as had never been before and has seldom been since. The editor included in the 64-octavo pages of his first few numbers news, foreign and domestic, history, philosophy, questions and answers, letters, poetry, music, translations, news of the learned world, "novels," essays, fables, and book notices — in short, every kind of material that had ever been proved of value in attracting and interesting readers. Even the wood-cuts were not omitted. Verses by Prior, Sedley, Mrs. Behn, Oldmixon, Dennis, D'Urfey, and Tate, jostled for a place beside learned disquisitions on "the Nature of Dryness and Moisture," or "a Description of the Kingdom of Poetry." More or less original features included a "Lover's Gazette," made up of advices from the City of Beauty, the Town of Pride, or the Commonwealth of Enjoyment.

But so many diverse elements did not necessarily make for long-continued success. The news dwindled to a perfunctory paragraph in the seventh number, and then disappeared altogether, with a kind of apology by Motteux for his ever having tried to compete with the many newspapers. Other sorts of material appeared less frequently, and the 64-page *Journal* became smaller, until it was less than half its original thickness. Publication was stopped in

---

[5] See the excellent article in the *Publications of the Modern Language Association,* XXXII, 22–3, by Professor Dorothy Foster, who makes much of the conditions in London at this time as explanation of the rise of such a journal in England.

November, 1694; or, at least, that number is the last preserved in the British Museum collection.

The *Gentleman's Journal* was one of the most important serial publications of the Century. Up to this time there had been among educated readers a strong prejudice against fiction or poetry — note the statements of De la Crose. Verses or works of " romantick " nature had been considered unfit for the perusal of the serious reader. Literary appreciation could not begin, nor could criticism develop, until such a prejudice was overcome. The *Gentleman's Journal* and its contemporary, the *Athenian Mercury,* had more influence than any previous publications in effecting and promoting the change. To what extent this is true of Motteux's serial, is shown by a reading of the tables of contents during the first few months. In the January number (1692) we find verses by Tate, imitations of Horace, a description of the Kingdom of Poetry, enigmas and an article on enigmas, dramatic criticisms, and songs with music. The February number contains verses by Prior, an article on *Cleomenes,* " a new Dryden tragedy," an essay on the friendly cheat, and a critical discussion of Perrault's *Ancients and Moderns.* Similar were the contents of each monthly number. Beginning with the third month, each number contained a " novel," while the interest in critical discussion is evinced by papers on Boileau, Dryden, on new books and plays, and on the need of an academy in England.

The first number of the *Gentleman's Magazine* (1731) which is generally regarded as the first magazine of a modern type in England, contained only one feature that is not anticipated by this work of Motteux's. Even the title is reminiscent of the *Gentleman's Journal.* And other miscellanies between 1692 and 1731 were, without exception, obvious imitations of this early work.

The first important imitator was *Miscellanies over Claret,*

" or the Friends to the Tavern the best friends to Poetry," (1697) a twenty-page monthly collection of poems, translations, etc. The author admitted his debt to the *Gentleman's Journal,* from which his own serial differed in being made up entirely of verse. In fact, it was the first *real* journal of poetry. The one number available contains two complimentary and patriotic odes, one satirical poem to the " Oxford Laureate," and an imitation of Martial.

The *Weekly Entertainer* (October 24, 1700) of which only one number has been preserved, not only supplies a further illustration of this tendency to wholesome amusement, but — what is more important — in form and content is one of the best anticipations of the later *Tatler* or *Spectator.* It was a large half-sheet folio, filled with a single essay — a dream narrative, not greatly different from those of Steele and Addison. A reforming aim is apparent in the essay.

The *Mercurius Theologicus; or, Monthly Instructor* (January to December, 1700) belongs here only because of its influence on a later miscellany. " Briefly explaining and applying all the doctrines and duties of the Christian religion, that are necessary to be believed and practiced, in order to salvation," it was devoted to religious propaganda, but the general idea of reform and its essay style connect it with the *Weekly Entertainer,* as another predecessor of Steele.

An important imitator of the *Gentleman's Journal* began in 1701, when Dunton first published his *Post Angel,* a monthly miscellany of about seventy pages. The one feature of the *Gentleman's Magazine* omitted in Motteux's journal is here supplied in obituary notices and articles. In the moral tone of the *Post Angel* is seen the influence of the *Mercurius Theologicus* of the previous year — a corrective tendency anticipating Defoe and Steele — while the variety of its contents allies it with the miscellany form. At the beginning the projector divided his serial into five parts:

1. Remarkable providences for the preceding month (36 pp.) [6]
2. Lives of the most eminent persons who had died the preceding month (21 pp.)
2. The New Athenian Mercury (4 pp.)
4. Publick news at home and abroad (6 pp.)
5. An account of books lately published, and now going to press (2 pp.)

To each part was added a "spiritual observator" in marginal comments. In July 1702, a new part was added for original poetry, and another section devoted to original essays "on all manner of diverting subjects," among which we find sympathy of souls, disobedient children, divine titles, and the Tower of Babel. Dunton's conception of "diverting" was evidently somewhat limited. In spite of the religious bent of the *Post Angel*, the combining of such elements as obituary notices, questions and answers, moral essays, and a catalogue of books, gives this serial a prominent place in the history of English literary periodicals.[7]

With Defoe's *Weekly Review*, the most celebrated periodical before the *Tatler*, we are not concerned except for the numbers between its beginning, February 19, 1704, and the issue of May 17, 1705.[8] These concern us very much for they contained the *Mercure Scandale*, " Advice from the

---

[6] *Cf.* Increase Mather's *Illustrious Providences*, 1684.

[7] *The Pacquet from Parnassus* (1702) appeared as a 32-page miscellany of verse, with a slight mixture of prose. Only two numbers are extant. These may be seen in the Harvard University Library.

[8] *A Weekly Review of the affairs of France and of all Europe as affected by that nation, with an entertaining part in every sheet, being the Advice from the Scandalous Club* — this was the full title of the first number. It later appeared as *A Review of the State of the English Nation*, and later still, *A Review of the State of the British Nation*. It was published at first, twice-a-week, then thrice-a-week, and was of 4–6 pages.

Scandalous Club, being a weekly history of nonsense, impertinence, vice and debauchery." The idea of an imaginary group was unquestionably borrowed from that of the Athenian Society, while the term " Advice " had been used in the same sense by several predecessors of Defoe. The Scandalous Club answered the questions of correspondents, and, in the words of Defoe, generally censured the actions of men. After the eighteenth number, Defoe dropped the title, which was an obvious reminiscence of *Le Mercure Galant,* and the department appeared as " Advice from the Scandalous (after the forty-sixth number, ' Advice from the Scandal.') Club." As its popularity increased, this department tended more and more to occupy the major part of the *Review.* In fact, its success spoiled the plan Dunton had cherished of issuing another " question-project," and forced Defoe to put out a 28-page monthly supplement of Advice from the Scandal. Club, beginning September 1704. On May 15, 1705, he announced that this feature would thereafter be omitted from the *Review,* and would proceed by itself, as a Wednesday and Friday *Little Review.* The " Advice " had been omitted for several issues before this announcement was made — evidently crowded out by matter of importance, although why Defoe did not add two more pages and include it, is an open question. His own words, are, " The Author, finding the Publick and more weighty subject he is now upon more than sufficient to take up all the room, both in his serious thoughts, and in the paper itself, had on that account for some time past, thought fit to adjourn the Diverting Part, until those more valuable matters were something over. But finding the multitude and variety of things before him not less pressing now than ever, and the Brevity of the paper not giving any tolerable dispatch, he has resolved, for the future at least, to leave quite out the said part, called Advice from

the Scandal. Club." This he followed by the announcement of the new periodical which would contain the " said
part."

The *Little Review; or, an Inquisition of Scandal,* " consisting of answers of questions and doubts, remarks, observations, and reflections," was begun June 6, 1705, as a
four-page sheet. The contents of the twenty-three numbers issued were similar to those of the earlier *Athenian
Mercury,* except that questions and answers were frequently
in the form of letters. Otherwise, it is the best example
after Dunton of the pure question-answer serial. As it
lengthened the queries into letters and the answers into
essays, it was an important link between the *Athenian Mercury* and the *Tatler,* as well as subsequent publications em-
ploying this device. The *Little Review* — and this cannot
be too much emphasized — was a direct descendant of Dunton's serial. It was a continuation, not so much of Defoe's
" Advice from the Scandal. Club," as of the monthly supplements that accompanied his *Review,* which consisted of
questions and answers almost entirely. Defoe's prefaces
show that originally he had no thought of becoming a
successor to Dunton in this particular, but the volume of
queries submitted to the Club forced him to issue first
supplements and then a separate publication. Defoe's characteristic reforming tendency is nowhere better exhibited
than in the answers of the *Little Review.* Although this
serial must have been a profitable venture, since it carried
from two to three columns of advertisements, Defoe's interest was apparently claimed for other things. The twenty-
third number (August 21) is the last now to be found.

So much has been written in praise of " Advice from the
Scandalous Club," that little need be said here. Defoe's
versatile and able pen refined the methods of his predecessors, and made more effective the old devices for entertain-

ing readers. His impulse to correct and reform carried on the tradition of Dunton's several periodicals and Tutchin's *Observator* of 1702,[9] and approximated very closely the moral tone of Steele. Drinking, loose language, the condition of the stage, gambling, war, love, poetry, the treatment of women — these subjects were grist for the mill of his active mind. It has been justly observed that the *Review* was superior to the earlier periodicals it derived from, both in the kind of entertainment it furnished and the style in which its contents were presented. More than anything else, the club idea and the spirit with which it made war on the vices and follies of the time, connect it with the works of Steele and Addison.

Defoe, when he announced the separate publication of " Advice from the Scandalous Club," promised readers of the *Review* a little diversion at the end of the paper. This was provided in the " Miscellanea," usually a discussion of some question of trade, theology, or popular controversy. The " Miscellanea " can be of little interest here, therefore, except as evidence that this periodical writer had accepted it as a part of his task to entertain readers as well as admonish and inform them.

As an indication of the taste of the times, an interesting " house organ " appeared in 1706. It was the *General Remark* of Charles Povey, published Monday, Wednesday and Friday, until 1708, in a large two-page form. It had a wood-cut, picturing a burning house, in the upper left-hand corner of the first page; indication, of course, that Povey's business was fire insurance. The publisher followed the plan of popular periodicals in his make-up and contents. A question and answer department, an article for the " curious," and an allegory or other entertaining matter, insured the interest of the average reader; while for the man of affairs

9 See p. 56.

there were exchange rates, commodity prices, and news of the arrival of the mails from distant points.

An important example of the influence of Motteux's *Journal* appeared soon after this, in the *Monthly Miscellany or Memoirs for the Curious,* " by several hands," and lasting as a thirty-two page monthly from March, 1707, to September, 1710. The desire to know, which had been fostered by the several serials of De la Crose and Dunton, and the desire for entertainment fostered by lighter periodicals, were here exploited together, although the entertainment furnished was limited by a very strict decorum. At the beginning of the first number, the unknown conductor said,

> The publick is desired to give their opinions upon the several enquiries following:
> Who was the best moral philosopher?
> Whether the existence of such a principle in the material world as gravitation be not the most natural demonstration of their being a God?
> Whence is the origin of ambergrease?
> Is nature preferable to art?
> What diseases are incurable?
> Who was the best poet, Horace or Virgil?

This was an original way of attracting readers brought up on the *Athenian Mercury,* " Scandalous Club," and *Post Angel,* and the articles in the numbers which followed should have done much to appease their desire for knowledge of recondite things. That this periodical was to be no *London Spy* was made clear where the reasons for including poetry were set forth thus: " The amusements of poetry will refine the conversations of the sullen and morose, and polish such a conversation as wants a mixture of gallantry and complaisance." A section of the *Miscellany* was therefore devoted to the muse, but most of the columns were occupied with learned subjects or the inevitable controversial divinity — either in the analysis and abstracting of books or in unsigned articles.

Yet the *Monthly Miscellany* deserves emphasis in this study because it is primarily a literary periodical. An essay on wit and humor, a treatise on poetry, dialogues upon literature and " critick," articles on books that had grown scarce, on the lives of philosophers, orators, poets, letters concerning tragedy, the academies of Paris, the character of Bayle's *Dictionary*, a dissertation on pastoral poetry, Dr. Bentley's emendations, a vindication of the Ancients against Perrault, a new method of cataloguing libraries, a new edition of Longinus, how to read the classics — these are representative of the subjects treated. It was easily the foremost literary journal of its time, in anything like a modern sense. The character of popular miscellany was preserved by lighter matter, such as " Advice to husbands of bad wives," a descriptive essay on the Amazon River, " characters," and travels in Persia.

A rival miscellany, started the same year, was the *Muses Mercury* (January 1707 — January 1708). The initial number of twenty-four pages contained poems by Tate, Manning, the Earl of Roscommon, and Steele, as well as Dryden's prologue for the *Prophetess,* Garth's and Dennis's prologues for *Tamerlane* and *Julius Caesar* respectively, an account of the stage, comment upon new operas and plays, a hostile discussion of Collier's attack on the stage, and notices of new books, including Congreve's *Poems* (then " in preparation ") and Prior's works. It has long been supposed that Steele contributed to the *Mercury,* but there is no actual evidence that this was the fact. Some elementary criticisms are notable ingredients in this miscellany. For example:

The *Opera of Rosamund* was performed on Tuesday, the Fourth of March; and the Town has by its applause justified the character we presumed to give it from our own judgment. The Harmony of numbers and the Beauty of the sentiments are universally admired. It has been disputed, whether the music is as good as that of *Arsinoe;* but, without entering into any comparisons, it must be confessed, that the airs of *Rosamund* are fine, the Passions well touched, and there being such a vast difference between the merit of the poems, the Dispute, 'tis probable, when decided, will be determined in favor of *Rosamund.*

It has been elsewhere shown that Addison's imitation of Horace (Ode iii, *lib.*, iii) appeared anonymously in this periodical, with a commendatory notice that would seem to establish Addison as a friend of the editor. Moreover, *Chevy Chase* was commended in the *Muses Mercury* long before Addison called attention to it in the Spectator.[10]

---

[10] *Mod. Phil.* VIII, 123–134 (see p. 124 note).

The Diverting Poſt.

From *Saturday* October 28, to *Saturday* November 4, 1704.

In Pugnam Blenheimenſem.

GErmanos, Bavaros, Gallos, Bellantibus Anglis,
Servavit, vicit, perdidit, una dies.

On the Lady SUNDERLAND.

By a Scholar of Fifteen Years of Age, at *Weſtminſter* School.

IN happy Days was Sachariſſa's Reign,
When Beauty ſhone, and did not ſhine in vain,
The Sons of Art could all her Charms expreſs,
And Rival Nature in the faireſt dreſs:
Vandike and Waller warm'd with equal Fire,
Touch'd the ſoft Canvas and the ſofter Lyre:
And the fair Nymph deſies the power of Times,
In Living Colours and Immortal Rhimes:
As Altrop now we ſee in brighter Flame,
And Sachariſſa ſtoops to Churchill's Fame:
But where's the ſkilful Hand that can preſent
Her matchleſs Form in Numbers or in Paint?
Arts that are reſiſt'd and cheriſht by the Fair,
By too great Excellency oppreſs'd, deſpair:
While meaner Faces Triumph over Fate,
Superiour Beauty has a ſhorter Date:
Yet happy Churchill that ſhe can't live long
In Kneller's Oil, or Hallyfax's Song.

By the Lady RUTLAND.

THE Beauteous Sunderland much brighter Shines,
In Hallyfax's ſoft and Charming Lines,
Than Sachariſſa did with all the Skill
Of fam'd Vandike, or happy Waller's Quill;
For tho' by Love and Beauty they were fir'd,
And ſeem'd to Paint and Write by Love inſpir'd;
They wanted Hallyfax's matchleſs Art,
With pleaſing Senſe their Paſſions to impart.

An Imitation of the Sixth ODE of *Horace*, beginning, *Scriberis Vario fortis.*

Apply'd to his Grace the
Duke of MARLBOROUGH.

Suppos'd to be made by Capt. R. S.

SHou'd Addiſon's Immortal Verſe,
Thy Fame in Arms, great Prince, Rehearſe,
With Anna's Lightning you'd appear,
And glitter o'er again in War:
Repeat the Proud Bavarian's Fall,
And in the Danube plunge the Gaul!

'Tis not for me thy Worth to ſhow,
Or Lead Achilles to the Foe;
Deſcribe ſtern Diomed in Fight,
And put the wounded Gods to Flight:
I dare not, with unequal Rage,
On ſuch a Mighty Theam ingage;
Nor Sully in a Verſe like mine,
Illuſtrious Anna's Praiſe, and Thine.

Let the laborious Epic ſtrain
In lofty numbers ſing the Man,
That bears to diſtant Worlds his Arms,
And frights the German with Alarms:
His Courage and his conduct tell,
And on his various Virtues dwell,
In trifling Cares my humble Muſe
A leſs Ambitious Trail purſues,
Inſtead of Troops in Battel mixt,
And Gauls with Britiſh Spears transfixt:
She Paints the ſoft Diſtreſs and Mein
Of Dames expiring with the Spleen.

From the gay Noiſe affected Airs,
And little Follies of the Fair,
A ſlender ſtock of Fame I raiſe,
And draw from others Faults, my Praiſe.

PROLOGUE for Mr *Wilks.*

SInce Churchill's Fame has thro' our Regions run,
All our Dramatick Heroes are undone:
Scipio and Hannibal can pleaſe no more;
Nor Cæſar Conquer on the Britiſh Shore:
Such Havock with our Heroes he has made,
That Alexander's ſelf afford no aid;
Tho' Rich by turns made all his Braves advance,
And loſt as many Generals as France;
Quite unemploy'd his Tragick Heaven ſtands,
And all his Gods lie Dead upon his Hands.

Who wou'd the fate of mighty Empires run,
When Sovereign Rich, with Lewis is undone!
When to ſuch low expedients Both ſubmit,
That One from Switzerland wou'd Armies get,
T'other from Dublin draws Recruits of Wit;
Eſtcourt, their Phœnix, he has brought to Night,
At any rate to purchaſe your delight;
To give you joy he does a Nation Sack,
For Ireland ſcarce will Laugh till he goes back;
Who tho' He's pleaſ'd with the Applauſe they give
His finiſh'd Fame, he wou'd from you receive.
Your Stamp muſt qualiſie each Grand Affair,
An Iriſh Act of Parliament and Player,
Have little force without a Sanction here.

CLA-

III

SOME CRITICS AND REFORMERS

IT has been shown that the development of what may be termed the " learned " periodical, on the one hand, and the serial of entertainment, on the other, has involved the beginnings of criticism in periodicals and the steady rise of a tendency toward reform of manners and morals. From the beginning, English literary periodicals were concerned with morals. The strict yet non-aggressive rectitude of De la Crose was supplemented by the pious and proselyting zeal of Dunton.

Among the serials omitted from the foregoing classification was Dunton's *Night-Walker,* or *Evening Rambles in Search after Lewd Women,* "with conferences held with them." It had a title sufficiently intriguing, but the reader looking for questionable entertainment is sorely disappointed to find that rambles and conferences had as their object the reformation of the women. For a similar design, one must go back thirty-six years to the *Wandering Whore* of 1660, a pamphlet issued for the same expressed purpose as Dunton's serial, and from which he probably got his idea. The *Night-Walker* was begun in September, 1696, a monthly octavo of 26 pages, selling for sixpence. Seven extant numbers preserve this curious effort to exploit the reforming trend of the time. Dunton's pious cant is more transparent in this serial than elsewhere. The originality of the project deserves some notice. Otherwise, the *Night-Walker* is worthless as a periodical, save as it illustrates the very general interest in the correction of morals which preceded the *Tatler*. Dunton's declaration of war on the "chief prostitutes in England, from the pensionary miss down to the common strumpet," and his expressed purpose "to expose vice monthly in lively colors and describe the dismal consequences, so as to frighten and shame women out of that life," whether dictated by religious or mercenary motives, added another impulse to the wave of reform.

The *Observator* of Captain John Tutchin, a folio half-sheet, appearing Wednesday and Saturday (1702) was mainly concerned with politics, like so many serials of the same general character. The ill-natured observations on plays and players in numbers 40, 57, 59, 78, 90, and 91, and the frequent employment of verse, usually of a political nature, give it some title to attention here. Between 1703 and 1704 it became a series of dialogues between a countryman and the Observator. Throughout Tutchin's life (he died in September, 1708, and the paper was continued by other hands until 1712, when it fell before the Stamp Duty) the reforming tone is constantly present. As one writer put it, Tutchin was always croaking for piety, a fact which makes his critical observations of very little value.

A third periodical, not otherwise mentioned in this study, applied in 1708 the reform principle to books. The *Censura Temporum* (January 1708–November 1710) a 32-page monthly, was concerned with the "good or ill tendencies of books, sermons, pamphlets, etc." in a dialogue between Eubulus and Sophronius. The author proposed to discuss only those books which promoted or opposed the interests of religion or virtue. The dialogue form thus carried from the folio half-sheet into a much longer publication is interesting, but only the reforming tendency shown gives the contents any value in the evolution of periodicals. Locke, Le Clerc, and Pierre Bayle are condemned frequently, because their ideas do not conform to those of the Anglican Church. No criticism of literature is found in the *Censura Temporum.*

But the one line of development most interesting to students of the literary periodical — the most important phase of this study — is the gradual evolution of the critical spirit in the discussion of books. Remote beginnings are found, as we have seen, in the notices in newsbooks as early as 1646, which gradually became extended into something more than accidental advertising of a publisher's wares. From such humble origins grew the book catalogue in the form of a serial like the *Mercurius Librarius* of 1668; while under the influence of the *Journal des Savans* and the *Philosophical Transactions,* extended abstracts with comment, and finally simple reviews were developed. It has been shown that the estimates of authors followed, earliest seen in the *Universal Historical Bibliotheque* of 1686. Then De la Crose in 1691 began to mark passages he considered best worth the attention of the pious and serious reader, and for moral reasons to ignore certain types of books entirely.

Isolated cases of criticism appear, usually more or less envenomed, as we have seen, in the *Mercurius Eruditorum* of 1691. An even more remarkable example, not mentioned elsewhere in this study, was furnished in 1692 by the *Moderator,* a half-sheet folio concerned mainly with political controversy. This serial began with little enough distinction, but the third number (June 9) was given over to an attack on Langbaine's account of the dramatic poets, especially Dryden. The unknown journalist defends Dryden, berating Langbaine in language worthy of Lockhart or John Wilson Croker. Of Langbaine's book, he says " never was a noble design worse managed," and then proceeds to defend Dryden from the strictures of the critic. Some of his remarks are worth repeating:

In your accounts of men confessedly great, you only tell us their memory will be dear to all lovers of poetry; or else their works will preserve their memory to all posterity, etc., without ever pointing out their beauties and defects, which make up the character of every author and distinguish him from all others. . . . There is nothing, for example, so courtly writ, or which expresses so much of the conversation of a gentleman, as Sir John Suckling, nothing so sweet and flowing, as Mr. Waller, nothing so majestick, so correct as Sir John Denham, nothing so elevated, so copious and full of spirit as Mr. Cowley. . . . They have each their proper graces; and which makes every one appear the individual poet he is.

The author of the *Moderator* quoted derisively from Langbaine's lives of the poets, to illustrate the error of his method. Returning to Dryden, he then made an effort to free him from Langbaine's imputation of plagiarism, by showing many examples (Beaumont, Fletcher, Ben Jonson, etc.) of the wholesale borrowing of plots — to justify Dryden's practice.

Moderator number four was filled with derogatory criticism of the verse which occasionally appeared in the contemporary *Athenian Mercury*. No further criticism is found in the few numbers available. In evident imitation of the *Weekly Memorials* of 1688, the author announced at the end of each *Moderator* his subject for the next week.

Only four numbers of the *Moderator* are now to be found, and it is likely that the critical genius of its author was soon exhausted. But the habit of criticism was finding its way into English serials, under the influence of the French, perhaps. Discussion of the Ancients versus the Moderns appears in the *Gentleman's Journal* of Peter Motteux, and essays of a sort on Boileau, Dryden, and other writers. Tutchin's *Observator,* 1702, comments on the absurdity of the prologues and epilogues at the playhouses, in a manner agreeable to the modern reader of these wearisome productions.

By 1704 criticism had become a common ingredient of the social periodical, as the " Advice from the Scandalous Club " or the pages of *Monthly Miscellany* or *Muses Mercury* well illustrate. Moral propaganda and partisan prejudice lie behind most of the early critical comment, of course. There was probably little or no effort to separate comment on writers from criticism of morals until long after this. By 1709 no periodical criticism of lasting value had appeared. But much of the pioneer work had been done, and the public had become educated to look for it, before Steele and Addison, in the *Tatler* and *Spectator,* wrote the first critical observations in English periodicals that the world has not been willing to allow to lie forgotten in libraries.

Note on Newspapers with Literary Features

It is conceivable that the magazine of literature and entertainment might have developed from the newspaper — an evolution from the occasional features used to attract readers or to fill up space. But such does not seem to have been the case. On the contrary, a study of the early newspaper press makes it clearly evident that the journal of news has always borrowed its features from the serials of literature and entertainment.

The earliest news sheet of importance which showed a deliberate aim to entertain readers was the *Mercurius Bifrons* (1680) with its page of serious newsmatter balanced by its page of " jocular intelligence." It has been already mentioned, as has the *Observator* of 1681, which also shows an effort to entertain; but a few other early news sheets need to be included in this category.

The first really good example of a newspaper with features was John Dunton's *Pegasus, with news, an Observator, and a Jacobite Courant.* It was a thrice-a-week half-sheet folio, "written in a different method from all other newspapers." It was begun June 15 and stopped September 14, 1696, after forty numbers had been issued. The "Observator" department was a palpable anticipation of the "observators" of the *Post Angel* (1701) while the "Jacobite Courant" was designed to correct the insolences of the Government's enemies and divert its friends. The "Courant" was at first written in verse. From June 29 it was written in prose. Notable contents were "A Short Character of Ambition," an essay in the manner of Bacon, Old Tredskin's "new ark of novelties," and dialogues between a Williamite and a Jacobite. Dunton's early intention to close the volume with the thirtieth number was carried out, and thereafter the "Jacobite Courant" was abandoned. Neither á distinguished newspaper nor a periodical of amusement, the *Pegasus* of Dunton is noteworthy as an early combination of the two.

Except for occasional verse in the London *News-Letter* of 1695 and the *Post-Boy* of 1698 (frequently used because of the lack of news) almost no other features are to be found in newspapers until the appearance of Defoe's *Review* in 1704, already discussed at length. In spite of Defoe's utterances to the effect that he saw value in giving readers entertainment along with their news, few or none of his contemporaries seem to have profited by his example. In fact, after the *Review* there was almost no effort made by newspaper publishers to divert or entertain readers, until the half-sheet folio form was abandoned generally for the four-page or six-page newspaper.

IV

THE *TATLER, SPECTATOR,* AND *GUARDIAN*

IN a restricted sense it may be said that everything in the evolution of the literary periodical in England leads up to the *Tatler, Spectator,* and *Guardian.* The moral emphasis of Dunton and De la Crose, the erudition of Oldenburg and Hooke, the wit of New Ward and Defoe, the miscellaneous entertainment of Motteux, and the increasing tendency to comment on books and other written works, reappear, transformed greatly, to be sure, in the most important periodicals of Steele and Addison. The question and answer of the *Athenian Mercury* becomes the letter-filled essay of the *Tatler;* the *dramatis personae* of the *Weekly Comedy* and the characters of the *Spy* and *London Terrae Filius* are refined into Bickerstaffs, Will Honeycombs, Templars, and Andrew Freeports; the contentious trio of the *Mercurius Eruditorum,* the later Athenian Society, the Scandalous Club, and the " Society of Gentlemen " develop into the immortal coterie of the *Spectator.*[1] Moreover, the genial observations and illustrations of Steele regarding the worth of family ties and the delights of conjugal felicity find remote anticipations in the advice to un-

[1] The early periodicals were naturally influenced by the character writing of La Bruyère, Earle, Overbury, and others, even more than the *Tatler* was. Kinship had long existed between the character and essay forms, since essayists found the character a convenient device for making pictures or lessons concrete and impressive. This is undoubtedly the reason why periodical essayists used it. Professor Baldwin has pointed out how Steele and Addison individualized, while still leaving characters general enough to be recognizable. He has also shown that Overbury's Country Gentleman has something in common with Sir Roger de Coverley (*Publications of the Modern Language Association,* XIX, 75–114).

fortunates in love in the *Ladies Mercury,* and the letters to husbands of bad wives in the *Memoirs for the Curious.* Manners and morals — matters of conduct and social relations — had long been subjects of discussion by writers. Dunton, in the *Athenian Mercury* of 1692, declared the reform of manners to be the great object of his work. Allegory and poetry and fiction, as elements in the diet of readers, are found predominating in the columns of the *Gentleman's Journal,* a generation before the *Tatler* appeared.

There seems to be not a single trait shown in the literary periodical of the seventeenth century that is not somehow illustrated in the *Tatler.* Defoe's *Review,* because of its popularity, superiority of style and contents, and nearness in point of time, may have exerted the most direct and tangible influence on Steele's serial. Otherwise, it is folly to attempt to decide which of the periodicals of Ward or Dunton, De la Crose or Defoe contributed the most to the creation of the *Tatler.* Each had a part in building up the tradition of which the *Tatler* was the result.

Steele began to publish his serial on April 12, 1709 — a thrice-a-week folio half-sheet, selling, after the fourth week, for one penny. By the close of the year it was more popular and more widely read, probably, than any other English periodical. After considerable miscellaneous literary work, Steele seems to have made this venture chiefly in hope of financial gain. Like Dunton, seventeen years before, he planned to make his periodical a coffee-house and tavern oracle. No doubt he received hints from the *Weekly Comedy,* 1699, and Ward's *Humours of a Coffee-house,* 1707.

"The Lucubrations of Isaac Bickerstaff, Esq.," Steele playfully characterized it, making use of a name which was already well known throughout England as Swift's *nom-de-*

plume in several pamphlets of 1708, one or more of which prophesied the death of John Partridge, the infamous almanac maker. Steele gave Swift such credit as was due him, and carried on the jest at Partridge's expense for some time. It is barely possible that the idea of making Bickerstaff an astrologer may have derived something from suggestions in the *El Diablo Cojuelo* of Guevara (1641).[2] Steele's Bickerstaff — "an old man, a philosopher, an humourist, an astrologer, and a censor " — proved a happy creation, and grew to proportions his creator did not dream of in the beginning. Of all the numerous family of Staffs in the *Tatler*, Bickerstaff was the only really essential character. The finished *dramatis personae* of the *Spectator* group were as yet unthought of. Moreover, the contents of the earlier *Tatlers*, in lighter vain at least, were not remarkable. The new serial began with materials not very different from those of the *Gentleman's Journal*, " Advice from the Scandalous Club," or the *Monthly Miscellany*.

Yet the *Tatler* had two distinct advantages over its predecessors. One was the attractiveness of its plan. Different sections were dated from popular resorts of readers, suggested by the datings in the *English Lucian* and *Ladies Mercury*, perhaps, but original in that Steele proposed to fix definitely the matter for each resort. " Accounts of gallantry, pleasure and entertainment," were to come from White's Chocolate-House; poetry from Will's Coffee-House; learning from the Grecian; foreign and domestic news from St. James'; and what Steele had to offer on any subject not readily classifiable, he included in a section " From my own Apartment." The five departments were not intended to be used in each number of the *Tatler*, but rather to be employed as occasion or convenience dictated. An important

[2] *Modern Philology*, 1921, 177ff.

advantage of the plan was its flexibility — the author's privilege of including miscellaneous matter of all sorts under the heading " From my own Apartment."

A second distinct advantage set the *Tatler* apart from all publications which preceded it. Steele and Addison were its authors, to say nothing of other able pens among its contributors. Aitken says the world owes Addison to Steele.[3] The latter said himself, " I claim to myself the merit of having extorted excellent productions from a person of the greatest abilities, who would not have let them appear by any other means."[4] Be that as it may, viewed from the standpoint of periodical history, the importance of Addison's help to Steele is probably greater than critics are now accustomed to admit, although he wrote alone only forty-two out of 188 papers,[5] and although it is probably true, as alleged, that Addison usually elaborated the hints he received from Steele, who was the creative genius of both *Tatler* and *Spectator*. His first contribution is believed to have been in *Tatler* 18, although not until the autumn of the year did Steele receive substantial aid from him. Yet this author of the *Campaign,* Fellow of Magdalen College, Member of Parliament, and Under-secretary of State, must have added appreciably to the prestige of Steele's publication. Moreover, he brought to it what Steele lacked — an excellent classical training. He contributed, in his treatment of men and manners, the philosophy and wit and observation of the ancients. Plato and Ovid, Theophrastus, Terence, and Horace, gave him hints and the material of sententious comment on human affairs, which impressed a public long read in the heavier serials of De la Crose and the works of classical authors.

[3] *Life of Steele,* i, 249.
[4] *Spectator* 532.
[5] Greenough grants Addison forty-five, although he questions some. *Pub. of the Modern Language Association,* (1916) XXXI, 640.

Steele began the *Tatler* with an avowed purpose to paint
virtue and vice in their true colors, a moral intention fore-
shadowed in his poem, the *Christian Hero*. Unostenta-
tiously moral and corrective the *Tatler* continued. Gradually, it took the world of conduct for its theme, dropping
one after another of the departments less congenial to its
conductor. Its tone was simple — conversational. Its air
was that of persuasive authority, free from dogma — an
air impressive to the readers of a day when men gave attention to any self-constituted referee in their debates, who
could speak to their convictions or point out their weak-
nesses with kindness and grace. So much has already been
written about this aspect of the *Tatler* that it would be
folly to add more here. A keen-eyed contemporary said
more in a few sentences than all the commentators since.
Gay in 1711 wrote of Steele:

Instead of complying with the false sentiments or vicious tastes
of the Age — either in morality, criticism, or good breeding —
he has boldly assured them that they were altogether in the
wrong; and commanded them, with an authority which perfectly
well became him, to surrender themselves to his arguments for
Virtue and Good Sense.

It is incredible to conceive the effect his writings have had on
the Town; how many thousand follies they have either quite
banished or given a very great check! how much countenance
they have added to Virtue and Religion! how many people they
have rendered happy, by showing them it was entirely their own
fault if they were not so! and, lastly, how entirely they have
convinced our young fops and gay fellows of the values and
advantages of Learning!

As Steele and Addison became more sure of their public,
the *Tatler* became more didactic and sententious.

Isaac Bickerstaff by degrees became Steele's most congenial character and medium. His motto, used from the
very first number — Juvenal's *Quicquid agunt Hominis*

Nostri farrago Libelli — was pertinent; and from the mouth of this interesting old gentleman issued " lucubrations " on a wide range of subjects. The arrogance of the rich, the simple pleasures of the poor, parental partiality, feudal prejudices, and the beauties of Milton and Shakespeare, were not beyond the observation of Bickerstaff; nor did he fail to find in them lessons for the average reader of the *Tatler*. Yet convictions were not pressed ready-made upon readers, in the controversial manner of Dunton refuting Anabaptists, or with the heavy Huguenot principle of De la Crose. Readers were allowed to glean what they would. Steele's Puritan seriousness was humanized by good taste and quiet humor. He found it his greatest pleasure " to trace human life through all its mazes and recesses, and show much shorter methods than men ordinarily practise, to be happy, agreeable and great."

On January 2, 1711, the *Tatler* was abruptly discontinued. To account for this sudden stopping, many students of literature have taken rather unnecessary pains. It has been said that the projector tired of his original plan — which is certainly the truth. But it must be pointed out that Steele always was careless of adherence to it. The contents of the letter from Will's were by no means limited to poetry and drama, nor were drama and poetry included only in this department. From the first numbers, there was no hard and fast classification of material. Actually — whether writing from White's, the Grecian, or Will's — Steele and Addison wrote discursively, touching on men and things in a way similar to that employed in the single essays of a later date. Even the newsmatter from St. James' partook of the essay manner, while the famous account of Marlborough's action (September 6, 1709) was not related in the news section, where it belonged, but in a letter dated " From my own Apartment."

Clearly, Steele and Addison, as well as other contributors, found it more congenial to write from this less restricted point of view. In fact, Professor Greenough has shown that nearly one half the letters in the *Tatler* were dated " From my own Apartment." From Number 100 to the end, other department headings were used infrequently — White's five times, Will's four times, the Grecian, which had never been much employed, only three times, and St. James' six times. " From my own Apartment," on the other hand was used steadily more and more — eighty-five times before the one hundredth number, and one hundred twenty times after. Moreover, from the one hundredth, there was a noticeable tendency for the authors to devote each number to a single letter, whatever the place of dating. In other words, each of the later numbers of the *Tatler* consisted of a single essay by a single author. The earliest containing a single essay is Number 48; the last divided number is 176. " Sheer-Lane," a new place of dating, appeared in the one hundredth number, to be used with increasing frequency, as time passed.[6] Nearly always these Shire Lane papers occupy an entire number. In short, the *Tatler* had gradually dropped those features least congenial to the authors, and as a result the " essay periodical " had evolved.

The decline of news in the *Tatler* was in no sense a result of Steele's loss of the *Gazette* editorship — a loss which occurred ten months before the news had begun to disappear from the *Tatler's* columns. There were plenty of precedents for the gradual dropping of news, as other features developed. News likewise disappeared entirely, or greatly declined in importance, in the *Gentleman's Journal* of 1692, Dunton's *Post Angel* of 1701, the *Diverting Post* of 1704–5, and the contemporary *British Apollo*.[7] Be-

---

[6] " Sheer-Lane " is used as a place of dating in a letter in No. 27.

[7] Something has been said by modern editors of the *Tatler* regarding

sides, the increase in advertising, and the difficulty in keeping news fresh and timely, in the face of much competition from the newspapers, were reasons enough for eliminating this department. Add to these the fact that the single essay type had become a favorite form with writers and readers. Richard Steele was enough of a journalist to give the public what it wanted.

Again, the decrease in news had little to do with the political views expressed in the *Tatler*. As Swift in the *Examiner* witnessed from his hostile viewpoint, it was the " From my own Apartment " or " Sheer-Lane " essays, in the later numbers, rather than the paragraphs from St. James' which were suspected of containing political allusions. After the one hundredth number, the news, when it did occasionally appear, was as often as not made the text of a literary disquisition.

Writers of the day who contributed to the *Tatler* are now pretty generally identified. Greenough names with some certainty Swift, John Hughes, Fuller of Petersfield, Steele's friend, a youth of sixteen at this time, of whom Steele afterward wrote in the *Theatre,* William Congreve, John Duncombe, E. W. Montague, and Anthony Henley. Charles Dartiquenave, the humorist, Arthur Maynwaring, and Temple Stanyon were possible collaborators.[8]

The *Tatler* established the essay periodical as a type; the

Steele's debt to the *Athenian Mercury* and the *Review* of Defoe. No mention has been made of any obligation to the *British Apollo.* Yet here was a notably successful periodical, begun a year before his own undertaking, combining news and verse and questions and answers (virtually letters). When the *Tatler* appeared, the *Athenian Mercury* had been stopped for twelve years and Defoe's *Little Review* for four years, while the *British Apollo* was Steele's to read three times a week. Any hints he took from this type of periodical must have come from his contemporary.

[8] Greenough, *Publications of the Modern Language Association*, XXXI, 640 (1916).

Spectator perfected it. The success of the *Tatler* was marked, but was evidently felt by Steele to have little relation to the original purpose of the periodical, which seems to have been hurried to a close. Steele had seen the possibilities of a daily essay. He was probably glad to end the *Tatler*, and thus free himself from all the obligations to readers, assumed under the old plan. On March 1, the first number of the *Spectator* appeared, little different from the later *Tatler*, except that it appeared each day, to " grow into the life of the reader like an intimate friend." It was concerned chiefly with morals and manners, each number developing a single theme — a clean-cut message, flavored with inimitable humor. The spirit of Bickerstaff, who scorned to be an inquisitor, although he admitted he was a reformer, was consistently maintained. Mr. Spectator stepped into the foreground at the very beginning. He furnished the daily essay with a concrete character. Later came other characters, now too famous to need discussion, who summarized in themselves all the worthy traits of the literary periodicals of the past — the observation, the curiosity, the profound learning, the romance or genial wit, and the interest in widely various human affairs.

The change from a thrice-a-week *Tatler* to a daily *Spectator* was justified in the results. At first, three thousand copies were printed. Later, the circulation rose to four thousand, probably — far from the extravagant estimates of some commentators, yet impressive enough if one keeps in mind the conditions in 1712, when, as Mr. Spectator put it, an average copy was read by a score of disciples. When the Stamp Act went into effect on August 1, the *Spectator* valiantly doubled its price and survived, although many other periodicals gave up the ghost. It was greatly handicapped, however, by the heavy taxes; and only a large amount of advertising enabled it to continue until

December 6, 1712. Steele seems to have been a very good business man, securing for his columns every sort of paid notice (not excepting those of quacks) then inserted in periodicals. Lewis thinks the short career of the later *Spectator* (June 18 to December 20, 1714) revived by Addison without Steele's help, was due to its inability to compete with newspapers for the advertising market.[9]

Among other elements derived to some extent from their predecessors, the criticism of the *Tatler* and *Spectator* is notable. It savored not so much of the heavy discussions of the earlier abstract serials as of the familiar criticism of nineteenth-century essayists. Steele's method is indicated in his remarks on Shakespeare. He could not turn away from him without "strong impressions of honor and humanity." Steele was informal and impressionistic, with no enunciated theory nor critical principles. When he attempted a methodical setting forth of his views, he used reason and good sense, the shibboleths of his age. Yet he was impatient of formalism. At his best, he allowed his individual taste to be its own justification. Like many a greater critic, he sometimes wrote ineptitudes and passed worthless judgments. But he is more often illuminating and suggestive.

Addison had something in common with Steele. Like the latter he opposed a narrow rationalism. A classicist by training, he was much more than a strictly classical critic. Like Steele he was led, to a great extent, by his own tastes, and enjoyed revealing to others the object of his own admiration. But Addison's criticism was more pretentious and analytical than that of his colleague. There is nothing among Steele's papers similar to the essays on *Paradise Lost* and *Chevy Chase*, or that on literary taste. It has been well said that in so far as they can be pigeon-

[9] L. Lewis, *The Advertisements of the Spectator*, N. Y., 1909, p. 64.

holed at all, Steele and Addison belong with the early Romanticists.[10]

The *Tatler* and *Spectator* were the supreme examples of the essay periodical type — the type which began with them. Many such serials followed, but none could compare with them in consistent moral instruction, simple yet finished style, genial humor, or influence and popularity with contemporary readers and with posterity. They are monuments of their age, not so properly a history as a set of pictures of the times — revealing by a kind of literary cinema the whole of English daily life; men and manners, the professions, the theatres, the trades, the homes. They show the prevailing sentiments regarding education, religion, politics, and literature. Almost every condition of life, pursuit, pastime, conversation, taste, fashion, vice, folly, and virtue appears. Nothing seems to be left untold. The reader becomes acquainted with the entire scene gradually, as men do with their own city and neighbors and friends, in the course of business and amusement.

The contributors to the *Spectator* are less easy to ascertain than those of the *Tatler,* especially as little effort has been made by scholars to distinguish between the earlier *Spectator* of Steele and Addison and the later serial of the same name issued by Addison without the help of Steele. Among the actual or conjectured contributors to the early *Spectator* were Dr. George Smallridge, Bishop of Bristol, Thomas Burnet, Bishop Francis Atterbury, Mrs. Oldfield, the actress, Dr. Samuel Garth, Mrs. Manley, Rev. William Asplin, Vicar of Banbury, James Greenwood, and William Harrison.

The success of the *Tatler* and *Spectator* begot a multitude of imitators — sincerest tribute to Steele and his colleague.

---

[10] Cf. Neumann's *Shakespearean Criticism in the* Tatler *and* Spectator (*Pub. Mod. Lang. Association,* XXXIX, 612–623.)

Nathan Drake, a century ago, enumerated 221 followers of these essay periodicals. His list is faulty, in that, not having seen the publications in their original forms, he included many that should really be classed as miscellanies. The biographer of Steele has furnished the titles of 121 English and foreign imitators.[11] Many of these followers of the *Tatler* and *Spectator* are well forgotten; but it should not be thought that all have deservedly sunk to obscurity, although it may not be possible to consider them here. Many were original enough to make a place for themselves in literary history.

But little originality or merit is to be found in the earliest imitators. In fact, unscrupulous efforts were made in several periodicals to exploit the reputations of Steele and Addison. On January 4, two days after the last of Steele's *Tatlers* appeared, another *Tatler,* printed and sold by J. Baker, began as No. 272, " with the character of Mr. Steele, alias Isaac Bickerstaff." This short-lived serial may or may not have been an attempt to dupe readers. But there is no doubt about the object of another, started two days later as Nos. 272, 273 — printed for Morphew, the printer of the original *Tatler.* Under the title was the statement, " This paper, which was not published on Thursday last, is now, upon better thoughts, resolved to be continued as usual by Isaac Bickerstaff, Esq." Accordingly, the first number contained what purported to be a further instalment of the " Court of Honour," continued from December 19, just as the instalment of that date was continued from December 5. A close imitator of Steele's *Tatler* in everything that could be imitated, the continuation survived until May 19, overshadowed and finally eliminated by the rivalry of another spurious *Tatler.* This third serial appeared January 13, 1711, printed for Baldwin, and with Wil-

[11] Drake, *Essays, Biographical, Critical, and Historical,* 1809, Vols. I-II. G. A. Aitken, *Life of Richard Steele,* 1889, Vol. II, Appendix V, 4.

liam Harrison for its editor. Congreve, Swift, and "Anthony Henley, lately dead," were among its contributors. This, like the preceding one, was put out as a *bona fide* continuation of the *Tatler* by its original authors. The efforts of the projectors to keep the public deluded regarding its real nature are worth remarking. Even the change of printers (Morphew to Baldwin) was explained in the preface as because of dissatisfaction, etc. The authors did not hesitate to introduce new characters, however, like " Humphrey Wagstaff, kinsman to Bickerstaff " ; and dated letters from the Young Men's Coffee-House and Channel Row, as well as from resorts already familiar to readers. Many of the papers are well written, as might be expected from the pens of Swift and Harrison. The former's sketch of Steele in No. 28 is important. But except for a defence of the theater in No. 31 and advice to dramatic writers in No. 36, little critical effort is shown, to make it valuable to students of literature.

In a similar way the reputation of the *Spectator* was exploited. The later *Spectator,* that of Addison, was discontinued December 20, 1714. On January 3, 1715, another volume was begun by William Bond, who obviously tried to make readers think it a revival of Addison's work. The initial issue appeared as No. 636, and the form and manner were closely followed. The spurious *Spectator* appeared twice a week, for sixty-one numbers. It is now remembered chiefly for the poems it contained, ridiculing Pope and Philips. In its reprinted form, it appears as Volume IX of the *Spectator.*[12]

The first number of the original *Tatler* was not yet three

[12] *A Tatler Reviv'd* "by Isaac Bickerstaff" (October 16, 1727 — January 15, 1728) and a *Tatler Revived* of 1750, the latter referred to by Johnson in the first essay of the *Idler,* were more or less unsuccessful efforts to profit by the charm of a title. Two numbers (Jan. 1 and 8, 1717) are extant, of the *Mercury or the Northern Reformer* of " Duncan Tatler, Esq." (Edinburgh).

months old when the *Female Tatler* appeared, by " Mrs. Crackenthorpe, a lady that knows everything." Phoebe Crackenthorpe is now known to have been Thomas Baker, who proposed to give the town another paper of this sort, on Monday, Wednesday, and Friday, ironically declaring in his preface that more ridiculous things were done every day than ten such journals as the *Tatler* could relate. Mrs. Crackenthorpe was represented as a great lady, who had twice a week an assembly of both sexes, " from his grace, My Lord Duke, to Mr. Sagathie, the spruce merchant . . . from the Duchess to Mrs. Top Sail, the sea captain's wife. . . . " The fictitious conductress said she would date *all her advices from her own apartment,* and in them recount the conversation of grave statesmen, airy beaus, lawyers, citts, poets, parsons, and ladies of all degrees. This conversation, she asserted, would range over books, removals at court, disputed law cases, prices of stocks, new fashions — " and the first long pocket that was seen in town, received its reputation from having been approved at Mrs. Crackenthorpe's Drawing Room."

Now it is obvious to the student of essay periodicals that Steele must have felt the competition of a rival who started with such a plan, and enjoyed such success as is indicated by the column and a half of advertisements which Baker carried from the beginning. How much the proprietor of the *Tatler* was influenced is a problem for some one to determine in the future. All that can be remarked here is that Steele was certainly stimulated to his greatest editorial ingenuity. In particular, the idea of dating *all* advices in the *Female Tatler* from " my own apartment " seems to have been very suggestive; for soon after the initial publication of Baker's serial, Steele began to use a similar caption more and more, finally making the *Tatler,* as we have seen, virtually a single essay, as Baker's essay sheet had practically been from the first.

Female Tatler.

By Mrs Crackenthorpe, a Lady that knows every thing.

From Monday October 17, to Wednesday October 19, 1709.

THERE are a sort of Whimsical People in the World call'd *Poets*, whose Delight, whose Transports, nay, generally speaking, whose Livelyhoods proceed from *Satyr* and *Invective*, from maliciously observing the little failings of the rest of Mankind, and from an unhappy *Genius*, turn'd to Scandal, improving 'em into the grossest *Asperdiende*: Some do it in *Comedy*, others by *Paraphras'd Translations*; some by downright *Libel*, and others more by *Panegyrick*. Lady *Fancy-ful*, who had the Vanity to think herself expos'd in the *Memoirs from the New Atalantis*, started the Question, What kind of Creatures are these *Poets*? They must be *unparallell'd* in *Religion, Loyalty, Chastity, Sobriety, all Moral Virtues, and Correct Qualifications*, as nice *Dress* and *Address*, a just and proper *Decorum*, in different Companies and Conversations, but above all in—— *prompt Payment*: That they seem to take an assur'd Freedom in lashing not only the imagin'd Vices of the Town, but the pretty, pleasing, harmless Affectations of our Sex, which divert our selves, and give Offence to no body. *Colonel Florid*, who so judiciously penetrates into Mankind, and with so much Modest Ease and Musical Eloquence, delineates not only particular Persons, but any Sect of People, that he bewitches our Attention, enter'd upon the Subject. His Notion of Poets was, that they are a *Chymerical* Tribe, but few Degrees remov'd from *Madmen*, who ought not be trust'd with themselves, but like heedless, rambling *School-boys*, have ev'ry thing provided for 'em, their *Bounds* set 'em, and their *Pocket Money* paid 'em ev'ry Day; they have no more Concern about their passing thro' the *World*, than if they were not in it, yet have a more refin'd *Taste* of *Dress, Equipage, Buildings, Furniture* and *Entertainments*, than all the *World* besides; they have *Cloaths*, regardless at what Price they buy 'em, and as regardless of discharging it; ride in *Great* Men's *Charriots*, sit at *Great* Men's *Seats*, and as their Wit and Humour are the Spirit of the *Table*, think the *Greatest* Men are oblig'd to 'em for their Company.——Stepping out of the Room to give some Directions, I happen'd to hear Mrs. *Loveless*, my Intimate Acquaintance, and as I thought my Friend, sneeringly cry,——Why, what is *Crackenthorpe* but a *Poetess*? The Company was alarm'd at the *Aspersion*, and Mrs. *Wiseman* wonder'd, how a Serious, Reforming Paper, tho' larded with Jests, Epigrams and pleasant Tales, cou'd bring me under that Denomination; but when I found the Dispute growing high, I bolted smilingly into the Room, and told 'em Supper was just ready.
——The Collonel proceeded, That *Poets* having a finer thread of Understanding, a quicker Apprehension, and more noble Ideas of Things than the Generality; they

are intoxicated with *Sublime Conceptions*, fancy their Bodies, where their Imaginations Soar, and in the heat of their Poetical Flights, discover the Lunatick in all his Shapes and Postures; a Poem well finish'd is to them beyond settling a nice Act of Parliament, they have no Plots but in Plays, and seldom any there, and a *Comedy* once brought to a full Third Night, is to them ——coming to a vast Estate: They have no Notion of Honour but in the Hero of a *Tragedy*, Friendship but for those who lend 'em Money, Sobriety after a hard Debauch, nor Regularity either in Thought, Deed, Time, Behaviour or Habitation; therefore when their Patrons bestow Preferments on 'em, knowing their Disposition for Business, they generally take Care they shall be *Sine Curee* And are these Creatures, says Lady *Fancy-ful*, that set up for *Observators*, that won't let one be a little particular in Publick Places to be taken notice of, but one's Character is in the next *New Comedy*, which perhaps is so Beastly a thing, one is n't able to sit it out; but Mrs. *Tire-quill*, who has the *Indisposition* of Scribbling herself, wou'd n't allow *Poets* to be so Contemptibly treated; she said, they were rather *Demi-Gods* than *Men*; that their Thoughts were *Supernatural*, and tho' their Mortal Clay over-animated for so small a Tenement, oblig'd 'em sometimes to *Terrestial Consabulation*, yet they more frequently convers'd with *Deities*; *Jupiter* gave 'em *Majestick Notions*, *Mars* show'd 'em *a Specimen of War*, *Venus* told 'em pretty *Love Tales*, and they had rather be inebriated with *Bacchus* in Imagination, than be really so with the most distinguish'd *Animal* below the *Spheres* : That such Persons, whose Writings make Mortals as Immortal as themselves, ought not to grovel about Worldly Cares, nor subject their Fancies, which are always upon the Wing to any manner of Constraint : That the thought Conversing with an *Author*, and perusing his Works, before they were blown upon by the Ingrateful World, was, next to happy Conceptions of her own, the greatest Felicity upon Earth. Mrs. *Tire-quill* was so Zealous for the Reputation of the *Hero and Thersian Tribe*, and grew so inspir'd upon the Subject, that she wou'd immediately have talk'd in Verse, had not Collonel *Florid* turn'd the Discourse upon a sort of miserable Creatures, call'd *Wou'd-be-Poets*; Wretches! that are in Business, *Tradesmen*, *Petty-foggers* and *Notary Publicks*, that might plod on in their Thoughtless Vocation, grow Rich, keep Coaches, and never think of the next World, yet fancying they have a Genius, leave their prosperous Knavery to write *Songs, Madrigals* and damn'd *Plays*, till they starve indeed, being shunn'd by their own Tribe, and laugh'd at by the *Kit-Kat Club*. These are an Incorrigible Crew, who, tho' they are punish'd with Poverty, and the utmost Contempt, ye

However the *Female Tatler* influenced him, Steele and his work prospered while Baker's serial declined. On November 4, 1709, Baker announced a change of plan. Mrs. Crackenthorpe gave way to a "Society of young ladies." Each number, from this time on, was Lucinda's Day or Artesia's Day, etc., until 111 numbers had been published. On March 31, 1710, the first important imitator of the *Tatler* gave up the contest. Evidently, the deserved popularity of Steele's *Tatler* was by this time too much for Baker. It is worth noting that the inferiority of the *Female Tatler* to its greater model is apparent in the coarseness of language and near-obscenity of much of its contents. Like the work it imitated, it was made up of letters, narrative, and allegorical lessons of various sorts; but the ironical style and the questionable taste in which it was written reveal, perhaps, why this and many other rivals of Steele and Addison failed to divide seriously their reading public.

Swift's jest, carried out by Steele in the *Tatler*, became a boomerang, when one who signed himself " Jo. Partridge, Esq." issued his *Titt for Tatt*, for at least five numbers (March 2-11, 1710), in form an imitator of the *Tatler*. It was designed to let mankind know, three times a week, what important news lies hid in the " supercaelestial " archives. The author was probably not John Partridge, but another who was having fun at the expense of both Steele and the astrologer. He declared he could not condescend to visit the coffee-houses for his news, since he was in direct communication with higher powers. He expressed a desire to examine whether the intelligences of " brother Bickerstaff " were conformable to the measures directed from the stars. Steele — he heard — was dead and buried in Lincoln's Inn! *Titt for Tatt* had advices dated from " Sol in conjunction with Venus," the " Symposium of the Gods," and similar imaginary places.

A group of minor imitators of the *Tatler* and *Spectator*,

most of them preserved only in a volume of the *Harleian Miscellany* at the British Museum, have no great value as separate publications but are impressive when taken together. The *Gazette a-la-Mode,* mentioned in *Tatler* 229 as one of the unscrupulous followers of Steele, began May 12, 1709. It was full of coarseness, and little calculated to attract the real readers of the *Tatler.* The advice of the projector, Tom Brown, to readers, " If you find me witty, damn me for a fool; and if I prove a fool I shall need none of your curses," conveys very well the spirit of nonsense that inspired it. In form, this serial followed its model closely, datings being from London, Oxford, etc. Five numbers are all that can now be found.

On August 22, 1709, appeared the *Tatling Harlot,* " in a dialogue between Bes'o Bedlam and her brother Tom . . . by Mother Baudy-coat." Three numbers are extant. In form, a small four-page sheet, it was issued Monday and Friday, and was obviously published for the purpose of parodying the reforming aim of certain essayists. " Drunkenness too often the effect of matrimony," " Marriage made a jest nowadays," and " The character of a drunken life, in a letter to Mother Baudy-coat," were among the engaging themes.

Another imitator, the *Whisperer,* October 11, 1709 (22 numbers) was evidently inspired by *Tatler* No. 10, for it was conducted by " Mrs. Jenny Distaff, half-sister to Isaac Bickerstaff," a character created by Steele. Still another, *The Grouler, or Diogenes Robb'd of his Tub,* January 27, 1711, is more interesting than either *Whisperer* or *Gazette a-la-Mode,* for it anticipated the *Grumbler* and the *Prater,* as an example of the adaptation of the single-essay serial to the development of a single trait or the correction of a single vice. From the title, one would almost expect the same specialization in the *Pilgrim* (February 22) of " Don

Diego Picolomini." But the pseudonymous author explains his idea — " As pilgrims content themselves with ordinary dress and food, so will I with an ordinary style " — and characterizes his publication as a delightful relation of many comical, serious, and remarkable transactions . . . the different figures of the pilgrim in various continental countries, " continued by journals with edifying morals," and " interspersed with valuable receipts, collected in his travels." Unfortunately, most of his receipts seem to have been obtained from quacks of the baser sort. The coarseness of the one extant number shows that the *Pilgrim* derives not a little from Ward's infamous publications.

The *Rambler* is chiefly notable for its use of Johnson's famous title. Only one number is preserved, No. 4, dated March 19, 1712. It appears to be a good imitation of the *Tatler,* for it contains a dream narrative, and a letter from " Jeremy Telltruth," which has in it a contributed poem. The *Rambler* was evidently issued on Monday, Wednesday, and Friday.

There is nothing especially original or notable about the *Miscellany,* the seventh number of which is dated June 9, 1711, the *Restorer,* August 17, 1711, the *Inquisitor,* June 26, or the *Surprize* " by Humphrey Armstrong, formerly Fellow of the Ancient and Renowned Society of the Seven Sleepers " (No. 4, dated Sept. 6, 1711). All were short-lived and in form closely modelled on the *Tatler.* The *Free-thinker,* on the other hand, five numbers of which survive, seems to be an imitation of the *Spectator,* for it contains well developed essays on manners. It appeared Tuesdays and Saturdays, from November 13, 1711. More important, in that they show the adaptation of this form to purely religious purposes, were *Serious Thoughts* (August 15, 1710) and the *Silent Monitor* (March 3, 1711).

Since periodicals were in those days, of all forms of property, the most difficult to monopolize, it is not surprising that a wide-awake printer of Edinburgh, James Watson, reissued the *Tatler,* some months later, for northern readers. Unfortunately, no copies of this reprinted edition have been preserved. But ten days after Steele's *Tatler* had ceased publication, Robert Hepburn of Edinburgh, a young advocate, set up another *Tatler,* similar to the London publication, edited by " Donald Macstaff of the North."

The *Examiner* (August 3, 1710 — July 26, 1714) inspired by the political aspects of the *Tatler,* but opposed to Addison and Steele in politics, was a work of Dr. William King, Mrs. Manley, William Oldisworth, Bolingbroke, Prior, Bishop Atterbury, Dr. Robert Freind, and Swift (who wrote 33 essays for it, and helped to conduct it). Like the spurious *Tatlers,* it throws much light on the activities of Steele and Addison. A critical comparison of the styles of these two essayists, in an early number, is especially interesting. On the whole, the *Examiner* has little value today outside the field of political journalism. But it gave rise to the (Whig) *Examiner* of Addison (September 14 — October 12, 1710) the *Medley* of Arthur Maynwaring and John Oldmixon (October 5, 1710 — August 6, 1711; revived March 3 — August 1, 1712) and the *Reader* of Steele (1714). Of these, the *Medley* was not wholly devoted to politics. It employed fable, narrative, and other forms of writing common to the moral essay. But its contents had not enough literary distinction to warrant longer treatment here.

The *Visions of Sir Heister Ryley* (August 1710 — February 1711) has been attributed on scanty evidence to Defoe, but was probably the work of Charles Povey. For eighty numbers, it appeared thrice a week, a four-page serial, consisting of " Two hundred discourses and letters representing, by way of image and description, the characters of vertue, Beauty, affectation, love, and passion; the agree-

ableness of wit, truth, and honour, made conspicuous
by morals, as also scenes of the Birth of Nature, the
sudden turns of fortune, the madness of domestic con-
tests, the humours of the town, and the false arts of life,
both human and irrational beings, traced through all their
intricate mazes." Just as these phrases of the projector suggest the works of Steele, so the plan of the *Visions* shows it
to be a close imitator of the *Tatler*. Essays in the first person, letters, and the other usual ingredients, were included
in departments dated from Will's Coffee-House, My Own
House in St. James' Square, From the Strand, From Tower
Hill, From Eutobia. The manifest effort to go Steele one
better — apparent in other imitators — is here very pro-
nounced. But like many other essay periodicals, the *Visions* failed in its content. Its matter tended too generally
toward the obscene and disreputable.

The author of the *Tory Tatler* (November 27, 1710) assured readers at the start that his title was only a term of
distinction, and did not indicate any intention of entering
into party disputes. He was going to confine himself to
subjects of pleasantry, humor, and morality — " at once to
divert and instruct my countrymen . . . and if I can get
money into the bargain. . . ." His frankness is at least
novel. The *Tory Tatler,* issued three times a week for sixteen numbers, was one of the closest imitators of the original *Tatler,* dating its letters from White's, the Grecian, and
" My Own Apartment," like the latter, with additional datings such as Drury Lane. Its essays approach the spirit of
those in the *Tatler* much less closely than those of the
Hermit (August 4, 1711 — February 23, 1712) or " a view
of the world by a person retired from it." The thirty available numbers of the *Hermit* consist of single essays with
such titles as On the old Cavaliers, On Burying in Churches,
On Discipline, On Good Husbandry, On the Abuse of Scrip-

ture to Perpetuate War, On Liberty of Printing. They show that their author had achieved in some degree the manner of Steele and Addison.

Other periodicals must be passed over without comment, but the *Rhapsody* (January 1 — March 8, 1712) deserves notice as an interesting variant of the type. The author's expressed purpose was to make antiquity live again by publishing essays on the life and works of the ancients. In a long preface, he draws what he calls the " landskip " of classic days, asserting that the reader, by acquainting himself with the ancients, may improve his judgment and his morals. The long, loose essays which filled the folio half-sheet, were, therefore, devoted almost exclusively to classical subjects. The *Rhapsody* was published thrice a week for thirty numbers. Considerable superficial criticism of contemporaries is to be found, and in later numbers the author became more and more absorbed in problems of education. To parents interested in the education of children, Ascham's *Scholemaster* was once recommended. Occasionally, the author resorted to filling up his two pages with translations from Plato or Sophocles. The *Rhapsody* is an excellent example of the wide variety of uses to which the essay periodical was turned.

But a rival half-sheet folio, started one month later, found a more original plan for popularizing the classics. The *Historian*, February 1, 1712, was made up of sections dated *Tatler*-fashion from various places such as Sparta, Athens or Rome. Each section consisted of some interesting classical story like the story of the Trojan War, or the Battle of the Romans and the Sabines, told as if by an eye-witness. Only a few copies of the *Historian* are available, so it is doubtful whether the design was carried on for any length of time.

" In pursuance of Her Majesty's most gracious directions," the *Monitor*, a thrice-a-week folio half-sheet, devoted itself entirely to themes of a reflective sort, for at least twenty-one numbers (March 2 — April 24, 1713). It was designed for the " promotion of religion and virtue, and for the suppressing of vice and immorality." It is unusual in that it was composed entirely of verse, much of it "performed" by Mr. Tate, Her Majesty's Poet-Laureate. The titles of the poems are descriptive — An Essay in Praise of Divine Poesie, An Exhortation to the Youths of Great Britain, The Upright Man, The Swearer, The Gamester, and the Day of Judgment.

The original *Spectator* came to an end on December 12, 1712. In the following March, Steele came forward with the *Guardian*, which, however, had been planned before the *Spectator* was concluded. The *Guardian* appeared daily for 175 numbers. Steele introduced a new plan and a fresh set of characters. Nestor Ironside, Esq., the fictitious conductor, declared himself " as regards the government of the Church, a Tory; with respect to the State, a Whig." But he felt that such age as his should have "nothing to manage with any person or party."

With this apparent profession of freedom from politics, the new serial began brilliantly. Addison is now credited with fifty-two essays of the total number. Fourteen papers are included in the collected works of George Berkeley. Pope, Thomas Tickell, Eustace Budgell, John Hughes, John Gay, Ambrose Philips, William Wotton, John Corey and Lawrence Eusden were occasional contributors. In spite of early professions, Steele was inveigled into political controversy, and on October 1, 1713, this essay periodical was brought to an end, to make way for a sequel, avowedly political — the *Englishman* (October 6, 1713 — February 11, 1714; revived July 11 to November 27, 1715).

The *Guardian,* while it continued, was a periodical not unworthy to take its place beside the *Tatler* and *Spectator.* Some idea of its popularity may be gained from the fact that in 1797 twenty-six editions had been published. Its design " to make the Pulpit, the Bar, the Stage, all act in concert in the care of Piety, Justice, and Virtue," was promoted for a time, by essays such as the Excellency and Superiority of the Scriptures, Grounds to expect a Future State Proved, On Sacred Poetry, Conduct of Certain old Fellows in Gray's Inn Gardens, and On the Tragedy *Othello.* Criticism of home and family was pleasantly introduced through the medium of the Lizards, clearly offspring of the Staffs in the *Tatler.* In the capacity of executor and guardian, Nestor Ironside acted rather as an intimate friend and relative — having as much anxiety for the successful issue of the Lizard affairs as a father would have had. His manner of educating Marmaduke, the son, and his conduct toward the numerous members of the family, were woven into a kind of criticism of common life. The chief entertainment arose from what passed at the tea table of Lady Lizard, or " Aspasia." The members of the family, their cares, passions, interests, and diversions, were represented, from time to time, as news from Lady Lizard's drawing room, a source undoubtedly suggested by the famous tea table gossip of Mrs. Crackenthorpe in the *Female Tatler.*

For its criticism, rather than anything else, is the *Guardian* valuable to students of literature. Steele's plea for tolerant and catholic criticism (No. 12), his wise advice about the difficulties of easy writing (15), his various animadversions on pastoral poetry, Hughes' praise of *Othello* (37), Pope's sly essay in which he contrasts Philips's pastorals with his own (40), the several essays on *Cato,* Pope's satirical receipt for the epic poem (78), to say nothing of references to Prior and Congreve, to Boileau and Longinus, and to various dramas then on the stage — these make up a not inconsiderable body of critical literature.

By 1712 the pioneer work in the field of literary journalism had been done. From simple book notices in the half-sheet folios of the seventeenth century, and from the more important abstract, had developed a kind of summarizing review, which, in the *Muses Mercury,* for example, appears not greatly different from the reviews of the nineteenth century or even of our own day. The gradual increase of poetry and crude fiction in early serials had led in the *Gentleman's Journal* to a miscellany or "magazine" type, which actually possessed in simpler form all the features of a modern literary magazine. Through numerous small serials preceding the *Tatler,* a roughly drafted single essay had appeared, which in the work of Steele and Addison became a finished literary form; and the essay serial, *i.e.,* a periodical containing a single essay, suddenly reached its highest development in 1711–12. The influence of the form extended over a century, but after 1800 the essay lost its identity as a separate publication and was gradually absorbed into the magazine or newspaper, where its growth and influence have been most important in determining the direction of literary journalism. The familiar essay, as well as the critical review, got its start in the days of Defoe and Addison. The important fact, however, is that every type of literary periodical which we know today had been created, or at least, had been suggested, in the periodicals before 1712.[13]

[13] One distinct type of periodical had not yet appeared — the "Magazine" proper, *i.e.,* a reprinted collection of works which had been previously published in weekly or tri-weekly serials. The *Gentleman's Magazine* is the earliest example of the type, but since it soon became a true miscellany, consisting largely of original matter, it is perhaps unnecessary to speak of it further. The *Monthly Review* and the *Critical,* which are usually regarded as the first reviews of a modern sort, really began as abstract serials, like the *Compleat Library* or *Works of the Learned.*

From the date of the *Spectator* there has been a permanent liaison between literature and periodical writing. Authors in Addison's day had become accustomed to thinking of the learned periodical or miscellany or essay sheet as their natural literary outlet. Defoe, Steele, Addison, Swift, Ambrose Philips, and Pope — these were out-standing figures in the periodical literature of the day. But a host of minor writers, not all Grub Street hacks, in scores of newspapers and other periodicals, were helping to mold public opinion, to improve literary taste, and to entertain readers with poetry and prose. Moreover, the education of the reader is also significant in this pioneer work of the seventeenth century. By the end of the century, Englishmen had acquired the habit of looking to their journals and monthly serials for a diet of poetry and fiction and essay. Literature had been popularized, as never before, and made accessible to the reading public of the day. Finally, critical journalism had passed through its embryonic stages and become a fully developed type. Periodical criticism of prominent authors and their works was henceforth to be part of general literary experience.

INDEX

Note. The titles of serials which have played some part in this history of the beginnings of English literary periodicals are printed in large capitals, and are followed by the dates of earliest publication.

Acta Eruditorum (Leipsic), 11*n.*, 12, 28

ACTA PHILOSOPHICA SOCIE-TATIS ANGLIA (*Philosophical Transactions*), 1665, 5–8, 15, 26*n.*, 27, 57

Addison, Joseph: Spectator Club, 16; debts to earlier journalists, 47; his imitation of Horace, 54; contributions to the *Tatler*, 64; and Steele, 65; his part in creation of single essay serial, 66; criticism of, 70; later *Spectator* of, 71; and Steele — their reading public, 75; Whig *Examiner* of, 78; his work and influence, 83–84

Advertisements of the Spectator, Lewis, 70

ADVICE FROM PARNASSUS, 1680, 37

Aitken, G. A., *Life of Richard Steele*, 64

Ames, J. G., *The English Periodical of Morals and Manners*, 10, 26*n.*

Ancients and Moderns, Perrault's, 46

Annesley, *The Character of Dr.*, 23

Andrews, *British Journalism*, 26*n.*

Apollodorus of Athens, 26*n.*

Arts of Empire, Raleigh's, 27

Ascham's *Scholemaster*, 80

Asplin, Rev. William, 71

Athenae Oxonienses, Wood's, 12*n.*, 16, 27

Athenaeum, 6

ATHENIAN GAZETTE (see *Athenian Mercury*)

Athenian Library, 22*n.*

ATHENIAN MERCURY, 1691: (main entry), 16–25; called first literary serial, 26*n.*, and *British Apollo*, 33; influence of, 46; predecessor of *Little Review*, 50; 52; verse of, criticised in *Moderator*, 58; relation to *Tatler*, 61; reform of manners the great object of, 62

ATHENIAN NEWS, OR DUN-TON'S ORACLE, 1710, 34

Athenian Oracle, 2*n.*, 22*n.*, 23

Athenian Sport, 22*n.*

Atterbury, Francis, 71, 78

Baker, Thomas, 74–75

Baker, James, 33, 73

Bayle, Pierre, 27, 53, 56

Beaumont, Francis, 58

Beaumont, John, 7–8

Behn, Mrs. Aphra, 45

Bell, Andrew, 23

Bentley, Richard, 53

Berkeley, George, 81

Bernard, Jacques, 11

Bernard, " James," 10

Betterton, Thomas, 42

BIBLIOTHECA UNIVERSALIS, 1688, 14

Bibliothèque ancienne et moderne (Amsterdam), 13

Bibliothèque choisie (Amsterdam), 13

Bibliothèque universelle et historique (Amsterdam), 11, 13, 28

" BICKERSTAFF, ISAAC," 62, 63, 65, 66, 69, 72, 73*n.*, 76

Blackwood's Magazine, 16, 33

BLOUNT, SIR THOMAS, 20, 30

BOHUN, EDMUND, 10

BOILEAU, 46, 58, 83

BOKER THE COFFEE MAN, 43

BOLINGBROKE, 78

BOND, WILLIAM, 34, 73

BOOTH, BARTON, 42

BOYLE, ROBERT, 16

BREWSTER, DOROTHY, 34

BRITISH APOLLO, 1708, 33, 35, 67, 68*n.*

BROWN, THOMAS, 24, 76

BROWNE, THOMAS, 2

BRUYÈRE, LA, 61*n.*

BUDGELL, EUSTACE, 81

Bureau d'adresse, 2

BURNET, THOMAS, 71

BURNEY COLLECTION, 40

Campaign, Addison's, 64

Cato, Addison's, 83

CENSURA TEMPORUM, 1708, 56, 57

Chambers' Encyclopedia, 10, 26*n.*

CHAUCER, GEOFFREY, 18

Chevy Chase, 54, 70

CHISWELL, RICHARD, 8, 9

Christian Hero, Steele's, 65

CLAVELL, ROBERT, 6

Cleomenes, Dryden's, 46

CLERC, JEAN LE, 10, 11, 13, 56

COCKBURN, JOHN, 14

COLLIER, JEREMY, 32, 53

COMPLEAT LIBRARY, 1692, 29, 30, 84*n.*

CONGREVE, WILLIAM, 53, 68, 73, 83

COREY, JOHN, 81

DE CORNEILLE'S *Dictionary of Arts and Sciences*

COUSIN, PRESIDENT, 4

DE COVERLEY, SIR ROGER, 39

COWLEY, ABRAHAM, 2, 18, 58

" CRACKENTHORPE, PHOEBE " (Thomas Baker), 74, 75

Critical Review, 84

CROKER, JOHN WILSON, 57

CROOK, W., 8, 9

CROSE, JEAN CORNAND DE LA: (main entry) 10–15; his serious purpose, 22; his *History of Learning,* 26; *Works of the Learned,* 27–28; relations with Dunton, 28–29; *Memoirs for the Ingenious,* 30–32; prejudice against fiction and poetry, 46; influence of, 52; his earliest approach to criticism, 57; moral emphasis of, 61; a predecessor of Steele, 62, 64; Huguenot principle of, 66

CROSS, MAURICE, *Selections from the Edinburgh Review,* 10*n.*

CROSSLEY, JAMES, 10, 26*n.*

CROUCH, S., 8, 9.

DARTIQUENAVE, CHARLES, 68

DAVENANT, WILLIAM, 2, 18

DENNIS, JOHN, 45, 53

DEFOE, DANIEL: contributions to *Athenian Mercury,* 20; his *Review* indebted to Dunton's *Mercury,* 22; relations with Dunton, 23–24; corrective efforts of, 28; *Review* anticipated by *Gentleman's Journal,* 47; (main entry) his *Review,* 48–51; his opinion of the value of entertainment in periodicals, 60; influence of *Review,* 62; his *Little Review,* 50, 68*n.; Visions of Sir Heister Ryley* attributed to, 79; importance of as literary journalist, 84

DEMOCRITUS RIDENS, 1681, 11, 37

De Re Poetica, Blount's, 30

DENHAM, JOHN, 58

El Diablo Cojuelo, 63

DIODORUS OF SICILY, 26*n.*

DISTAFF, MRS. JENNY, 76

DIVERTING POST, 1704, 42, 67

Dowley, James, 20

Drake, Nathan, 72

Dryden, John, 5, 45, 53, 57, 58

Dunton, John: his *Athenian Mercury* (main entry) 16–25; 50; relations with De la Crose, 28–29; his *Athenian News*, 34; his *Post Angel*, 47, 48, 67; fostered desire to know, 52; his *Pegasus with News*, 59–60*n.*, moral emphasis of, 61; precursor of Steele, 62; controversial manner of, 66

Dunton, Life and Errors of John, 16*n.*, 20, 21*n.*, 23*n.*, 28

D'Urfey, Thomas, 45

Earle, Thomas, Character writing of, 61*n.*

Edict of Nantes, Revocation of, 11

Encyclopedia Britannica, 10

English Lucian, 1698, 39–41, 43

Englishman, 1713, 82

Entretiens sérieuses et galantes, 28

Eusden, Laurence, 82

Examiner, 1710, 68, 78

Examiner (Whig) of Addison, 1710, 78

Fables, L'Estrange's, 27

Faithorne, Henry, 8, 9

Female Tatler, 1709, 74–75, 82

Fletcher, John, 58

Foster, Dorothy, 45*n.*

Free-Thinker, 1711, 77

Freind, Robert, 78

French Mountbank, 36

Fuller of Petersfield, 68

Gallois, Abbé, 4

Garth, Samuel, 30, 53, 71

Gay, John, 65

Gazette (London), 67

Gazette (Paris), 3

Gazette à-la-Mode, 1709, 76, 77

General Remark, 1706, 51

Gentleman's Journal, 1692, 30, 44, 47, 58, 62, 63, 67, 83

Gentleman's Magazine, 1731, 22, 33, 47, 84

Gibbon, Edward, 2

Gildon, Charles, 16*n.*, 20*n.*

Il Giornali de' Letterati (Rome and Paris), 12, 28

Grecian Coffee-House, 63, 66, 79

Greenough, Professor C. N., 64*n.*, 67, 68*n.*

Greenwood, James, 71

Grouler, or Diogenes Robb'd of His Tub, 1711, 77

Grumbler, The, 77

Guardian, 1713, 61, 81–3

Guerava, *Il Diablo Cojuelo* of, 63

Haley, Edmund, 7

Halifax, Marquis of, 20

Hanover Spy, The, 24

Harleian Miscellany, 36*n.*, 76

Harris, John, 40

Harrison, William, 71, 73

Hedges, Sir William, 20

Hédouville, M. de, 4

Henley, Anthony, 68, 73

Hepburn, Robert, 78

Heraclitus Ridens, or a Discourse Between Jest and Earnest, 1681, 37

Hermit, The, 1711, 80

Hill, Aaron, 34

Historian, The, 1712, 80

Historie des Ouvrages des Savans, 32

History of the Athenian Society, Gildon's, 16

History of Learning, 1691, 26, 28

History of Learning, 1694, 31

History of the Works of the Learned, 1699, 32

Hooke, Robert, 7, 9

Horace, 46, 52, 54, 64

Hughes, John, 68, 81, 83

HUMOURS OF THE COFFEE HOUSE, 1707, 43, 62

Idler, Johnson's, 74n.
INFALLIBLE ⁻ ASTROLOGER, 1700, 41
Introduction to the History of England, 31
INQUISITOR, 1711, 77

JESTING ASTROLOGER, 1700, 41n.
JOHNSON, SAMUEL, 74n., 77
JONSON, BEN, 58
JOURNAL DES SAVANS, 1665, 2, 3, 5, 8, 9, 11, 12, 14, 26n., 28, 57
JOVIAL MERCURY, 1693, 25
Julius Caesar, Shakespeare's, 53
JUVENAL, 65

KERSEY, JOHN, 8
KING, DR. WILLIAM, 78

LACEDEMONIAN MERCURY, 1692, 24
LADIES MERCURY, 1694, 25, 34, 62, 63
LANGBAINE, GERARD, 57–58
LATIN COFFEE HOUSE, 25
LE CLERC, JEAN, 10, 11, 13
L'ESTRANGE, ROGER, 27, 37, 38
Letter sent from Rome, A, by John Taylor, 16n.
LEWIS, L., *The Advertisements of the Spectator,* 70
Literary Gazette, 6
LITTLE REVIEW, 1705, 23, 49, 50
LOCKE, JOHN, 56
LOCKHART, JOHN GIBSON, 4, 57
LONDON MERCURY, 1692, 24
LONDON NEWS–LETTER, 1695, 60
LONDON SPY, 1698, 39, 52, 61
LONDON TERRAE FILIUS, 1707, 43, 61
LONGINUS, 53, 83
LORET, JEAN, 37

Magnalia Dei Anglicana, 1
MAN IN THE MOON, 1649, 36
MANLEY, DELARIVIÈRE, 71, 78
MARLBOROUGH, DUKE OF, 66
MATHER, COTTON, 19n.
MATHER, INCREASE, 48
MATY, MATTHEW, 5
MAUNSELL, ANDREW, 6
MAYNWARING, ARTHUR, 68, 78
MEDLEY, THE, 1710, 78
Mémoires of Frederic Maurice, 32
MEMOIRS FOR THE CURIOUS, 1701, 33, 62
MEMOIRS FOR THE INGENIOUS, 1693, 30
MEMOIRS FOR THE INGENIOUS, OR UNIVERSAL MERCURY, 1694, 31
Mercure Galant, Le, 1673, 44, 45, 49
MERCURIUS BIFRONS, OR THE ENGLISH JANUS, 1681, 16n., 37, 38, 59
MERCURIUS BRITANNICUS, 1626, 1
MERCURIUS DEMOCRITUS, 1652, 36
MERCURIUS ELENCTICUS, 1647, 36
MERCURIUS ERUDITORUM, 1691, 15, 16, 57, 61
MERCURIUS FUMIGOSUS, OR SMOKING NOCTURNALL, 1654, 36, 39
MERCURIUS INFERNUS, 1681, 37
MERCURIUS JOCOSUS, 1654, 36
MERCURIUS LIBRARIUS, 1668, 6, 26n., 57
MERCURIUS LIBRARIUS, 1680, 7
MERCURIUS MEDICUS, 1647, 36
MERCURIUS MELANCHOLICUS, 1647, 36
MERCURIUS MORBICUS, 1647, 36
MERCURIUS MUSICUS, 1699, 42n.

MERCURIUS PHRENETICUS, 1652, 36
MERCURIUS THEOLOGICUS, 1700, 47
MERCURY, OR THE NORTHERN REFORMER, 1717, 74n.
MERRY MERCURY, OR THE FARCE OF FOOLS, 1700, 41
MÉZERAY, FRANÇOIS DE, 3
MILTON, JOHN, 2, 18, 66
MISCELLANEOUS LETTERS, 1694, 31
MISCELLANIES OVER CLARET, 1697, 46
MISCELLANY, THE, 1711, 77
MODERATOR, THE, 1692, 57, 58
Modern Language Association of America, Publications of, 45n., 61n., 64n., 68n., 71n.
Modern Philology, 54n., 63n.
MOMUS RIDENS, 1690, 38, 41
MONITOR, THE, 1713, 81
MONTAGUE, E. W., 68
MONTHLY MISCELLANY, OR MEMOIRS FOR THE CURIOUS, 1707, 52, 53, 59, 63
Monthly Review, 1749, 84n.
MOTTEUX, PETER ANTHONY: contributed to *Athenian Mercury,* 20; *Gentleman's Journal* of, 30; his periodical work (main entry), 44–46; influence of, 52; his criticism in *Gentleman's Journal,* 58
Muse Historique, 1651, 37
Muses Cabinet, 37
MUSES MERCURY, 1707, 53, 54, 59, 83
Myriobiblion, 4

NEDHAM, MARCHAMONT, 2
NEWS FROM HELL, 1647, 36
NEWS FROM PARNASSUS (*Advice from Parnassus*), 1680, 37
NEWS FROM THE LAND OF CHIVALRY, 1681, 37, 38
NEUMANN, J. H., *Shakespearean Criticism in the Tatler and Spectator,* 71n.

NICHOLS, JOHN, 26n.
NIGHT-WALKER, 1696, 41, 55
" NOCTES AMBROSIANAE," 16
NORRIS, DR. JOHN, 17
NORTH, CHRISTOPHER (John Wilson), 4
Notes and Queries, 15
Nouvelle Biographie Générale, 11n.
Nouvelle de la République des Lettres, 1684, 11n., 27

OBSERVATOR, L'Estrange's, 1681, 38, 59
OBSERVATOR, Tutchin's, 1702, 51, 56, 58
OLDENBURG, HENRY, 5, 6, 7, 9, 30
OLDFIELD, MRS., 71
OLDISWORTH, WILLIAM, 78
OLDMIXON, JOHN, 45
Othello, 82, 83
OVERBURY, Character writing of, 61n.
OVID, 64

PACQUET FROM PARNASSUS, 1702, 48
Paradise Lost, 70
PARKES, SAMUEL, 10, 26n.
PARTRIDGE, JOHN, 40, 41, 63, 75
PECKE, SAMUEL, 1
PEGASUS WITH NEWS, 1696, 59–60
Pennyless Parliament of Threadbare Poets; or, All Mirth and Witty Conceits, 36
PERFECT DIURNALL OF THE PASSAGES IN PARLIAMENT, 1646, 1
PERRAULT, *Ancients and Moderns,* 46, 53
PETIVER, JAMES, 8
PHILIPS, AMBROSE, 73, 81, 83, 84
PHILIPS, SAMUEL, 43
PHILOSOPHICAL TRANSACTIONS OF THE ROYAL SOCIETY, 1665, 5–8, 15, 26n., 27, 57
PHOTIUS OF GREECE, 4

PILGRIM, THE, 1712, 77

PLAIN DEALER, 1717, 34

PLAYFORD, HENRY, 42

PLUTARCH'S *Lives,* 31

POETICAL COURANT, 1706, 43

POOR ROBIN'S OCCURRENCES AND REMARKS, 1688, 38

POPE, ALEXANDER: ridiculed in later *Spectator,* 73; contributor to *Guardian,* 81; his essay on Philip's pastorals, 83; 84

POPLAR, D., 32

POST ANGEL, 1701, 47–48, 52, 60, 67

POST–BOY, 1698, 60

POVEY, CHARLES, 51, 79

Prater, The, 77

PRATT, SIR PETER, 20

PRIOR, MATTHEW, 45, 46, 53, 78, 83

Prophetess, Dryden's prologue for, 53

PUBLICK INTELLIGENCER, 1654, 2

Publications of the Modern Language Association of America, 45n., 61n., 64n., 68n., 71

Quarterly Journal of Science, Literature and the Arts, 26n.

QUEVEDO, *Sueños* of, 37

RALEIGH, WALTER, 27

RAMBLER, THE, 1712, 77

RAMBLES AROUND THE WORLD, OR THE TRAVELS OF KAINOPHILOS, 1689, 38

RAWLINSON MANUSCRIPTS, 17n., 23n., 24n.

READER, THE, 1714, 78

Reflections on Ancient and Modern Learning, 31

Reformed Gentleman, The, 30

RENAUDOT, THÉOPHRASTE, 3

RESTORER, THE, 1711, 77

REVIEW OF THE AFFAIRS OF FRANCE, etc., 1704, 22; (main entry) 48–50; 60, 62, 68n.

RHAPSODY, THE, 1712, 80

RYMER, THOMAS, 30

RICHARDSON, CHARLES, 20

RIDPATH, GEORGE, 32

ROQUE, ABBÉ LA, 4

ROSCOMMON, EARL OF, 53

ROYAL SOCIETY, 5, 6, 7, 30

SAINTSBURY, GEORGE, 26

ST. JAMES COFFEE-HOUSE, 63, 66, 68

SALLO, DENIS DE, 3, 4, 67

SAULT, RICHARD, 17, 28, 30

Second Defence of the Short View, etc., Collier's, 32

SECRET MERCURY, 1710, 41

SEDLEY, CHARLES, 45

SERIOUS THOUGHTS, 1710, 78

SHAKESPEARE, WILLIAM, 18, 66

SHEAR, trans. of *Polybius,* 30

Short View of Tragedy, Rymer's, 30

SILENT MONITOR, 1711, 78

SLARE, FREDERICK, 7

SMALLRIDGE, DR. GEORGE, 71

SMITH, EDWARD, 23

SOUTHWELL, SIR ROBERT, 30

SPECTATOR, 1711: characters of, 40; pioneer work done before, 59; evolution of, 61, 63; Steele, creative genius of, 64; beginning of (main entry), 68–84

SPECTATOR, Addison's, 1714, 70

SPECTATOR, Bond's, 1715, 73

SPENSER, EDMUND, 18

Sphinx Theologica Philosophica, 1636, 16n.

Sportive Wit, or the Muses Merriment, 37

STAMP ACT, 56, 69

STANYON, TEMPLE, 68

STARKEY, JOHN, 6

STATIONERS COMPANY, 29

STEELE, RICHARD: Spectator Club of Addison and, 16; letters of, 25; corrective efforts of, 28; *Weekly Entertainer* a precursor of his work, 47; poems by, in *Muses Mercury,* 53; influence on criticism, 59; *Tatler, Spectator,* and *Guardian* of (main entry), 61–84

STRANGE AND WONDERFUL NEWS FROM NORWICH, THE, 1681, 37

SURPRIZE, THE, 1711, 77

SWIFT, JONATHAN: opinion of the Athenian Society, 20; his *Ode* on Athenian Society, 21*n.;* Partridge, the butt of, 41; his use of "Bickerstaff," 62; Steele gave him credit for the name, 63; his views of the *Tatler,* 68; wrote for Harrison's *Tatler,* 73; wrote for Tory *Examiner,* 78; an out-standing journalist, 84

Tamerlane, 53

TATE, NAHUM, 20, 45, 46, 63, 81

TATLER, 1709, Steele's letters in, 25; influence of *British Apollo* on, 34; features later copied by *British Apollo,* 35; form of *Momus Ridens* much like, 38; *English Lucian* precursor of, 39; *Secret Mercury* suggestive of, 41; anticipated by *Weekly Entertainer,* 47; *Little Review,* a link between *Athenian Mercury* and, 50; general interest in morals that preceded, 56; criticism in, 59; beginning of and influence (main entry), 61–84; Edinburgh edition of, 78

TATLER (Baker's), 1711, 72

TATLER (printed by Morphew), 1711, 72

TATLER (Harrison's), 1711, 73

TATLER (Edinburgh), 1712, 78

TATLER REVIV'D, 1727, 73*n.*

TATLER REVIVED, 1750, 73*n.*

TAYLOR, JOHN, 16*n.,* 36

TEMPLE, SIR WILLIAM, 20, 27

TERENCE, 64

TERM CATALOGUE OF THE LONDON BOOKSELLERS, 6, 7, 15, 23

THEATRE, THE, 1720, 68

THEOPHRASTUS, 64

TICKELL, THOMAS, 81

TITT FOR TATT, 1710, 75

TORY TATLER, 1710, 79

Tryals of Several Witches Lately Executed in New England, 19*n.*

TUTCHIN, JOHN, 51, 56, 58

UNIVERSAL HISTORICAL BIB-LIOTHEQUE, 1686, 10–14, 57

VIRGIL, 52

VISIONS OF SIR HEISTER RYLEY, 1710, 79

WAGSTAFF, HUMPHREY, 73

WALLER, EDMUND, 18, 58

WALTON, IZAAK, 2

WANDERING SPY, 1705, 43–44

Wandering Whore, 55

WARD, EDWARD: his *London Spy,* 39; *Weekly Comedy,* 40, 41; *Humours of the Coffee-House,* 43; *London Terrae Filius,* 43; *Jesting Astrologer,* a follower of Ward's publications, 41*n., Pilgrim,* resembles, 77; also 62

WATSON, JAMES, 32, 78

WEEKLY COMEDY, 1699, 40, 42, 43, 61, 62

WEEKLY DISCOVERER STRIPP'D NAKED, 1681, 37

WEEKLY DISCOVERY, 1681, 37

WEEKLY ENTERTAINER, 1700, 47

WEEKLY MEMORIALS, 1688, 14, 58

WEEKLY MEMORIALS FOR THE INGENIOUS, 1682, 8, 26*n.*

WEEKLY MEMORIALS FOR THE INGENIOUS, 1682 (another), 8

WEEKLY REVIEW OF THE AFFAIRS OF FRANCE, etc., 1704, 47–51, 62

WESLEY, JOHN AND CHARLES, 17

WESLEY, SAMUEL, 17, 23, 28
WHISPERER, THE, 1709, 76–77
WHITE'S CHOCOLATE-HOUSE, 63, 66, 67, 79
WILKS, ROBERT, 42
WILL'S COFFEE-HOUSE, 63, 66, 67
WOOD, ANTHONY À, 12, 27

WOOLEY, R., 29
WORKS OF THE LEARNED, 1691, 11, 27–30, 32, 84n.
WOTTON, WILLIAM, 31, 81

Young Student's Library, 22n.